Law & Hoarders

Organized Crime and Corruption in Haiti

Woodger Faugas

Citadel Press Academic Publishing

Published in the United States, by Citadel Press Academic Publishing.

Faugas, Woodger

Law and Hoarders

Hardcover ISBN: 979-8-9875566-5-8

E-book ISBN: 978-0-578-26744-9

Paperback ISBN: 979-8-9875566-6-5

DOI: 10.6084/m9.figshare.25565829

Contents

Chapter 1

Initialisms or Acronyms

BNRSV: Bureau National de Réparation des Sociétaires Victims (National Reparations Bureau for CEC Victims)

BPH: Banque Populaire Haïtienne (Popular Bank of Haïti)

CASECs: Conseils d'Administration des Sections Communales (Administrative Boards of Communal Sections)

CD: Convergence Démocratique (Democratic Convergence)

CEC: Coopératives d'Épargne et de Credit (Credit Unions)

CEP: Conseil Electoral Provisoire (Provisional Electoral Council)

CNLBA: Comité National de Lutte contre le Blanchiment des Avoirs (National Committee for the Fight against Money Laundering)

COCSOBFO: Coopérative de Consommation Soleil Brillant Fond'Oie (Consumer Cooperative of the Shining Sun of Fond'Oie)

CPI: Corruption Perception Index

EU: European Union

Fad'H: Forces Armées d'Haïti (Armed Forces of Haïti)

FAD: Fondation Aristide pour la Démocratie (Aristide Foundation for Democracy)

FL: Fanmi Lavalas (Lavalas Family)

FNCD: Front National pour le Changement et la Démocratie (National Front for Change and Democracy)

GoH: Government of Haïti

ICAC: Independent Commission Against Corruption MINUSTAHUnited Nations Stabilization Mission in Haiti

NGOs: Non-governmental Organizations

OAS: Organization of American States

ONA: Office National d'Assurance Vieillesse (National Office of Old-Age Insurance) PAC ModelPrincipal-Agent-Client Model

PFM: Public Finance Management

PNd'H: Police Nationale d'Haïti (National Police of Haïti)

PSM: Public Sector Management SOCABANKSociété Caraïbéenne de Banque (Caribbean Banking Society)

TI: Transparency International

ULCC: Unité de Lutte Contre la Corruption (Combat Unit against Corruption)

UN: United Nations

USD: U.S. Dollars

UCREF: Unité Centrale de Renseignements Financiers (Central Financial Enquiry Unit)

WB: World Bank

Chapter 2
Introduction

Since defeating the French more than two hundred years ago, Haïti has been a very unstable country. Throughout its existence as a sovereign nation, turbulent, revolutionary currents —in conjunction with French, Canadian, and American influence —have subjected its governments to more than thirty coups d'état and have led to the murder of many of its citizens and public servants. Furthermore, owing in part to France's imposition of a sizeable indemnity on the country's national treasury, Haïti has suffered from underdevelopment. The lack of economic opportunities and public goods available to its citizens has, in part, engendered a political culture that is ruled by decadence and various types of corruption, including but not limited to: cronyism, bribery, extortion, embezzlement, and nepotism.

Several years ago, in an attempt to reduce governmental corruption and promote public accountability and transparency, Boniface Alexandre —acting as the head of Haïti's provisional government from 2004 to 2006 —instituted by decree a semi-autonomous Combat Unit against Corruption named *Unité de Lutte Contre la Corruption* (ULCC). Established under the oversight of the Minister of Economy and Finance, this agency had a multipart mission. It aimed to: 1) protect public and communal goods; 2) ensure the efficacy of measures and actions in order to prevent, detect, punish, and eliminate corruption and related offenses; 3) encourage transparency in the management of public affairs; 4) promote private investment by establishing a climate of trust; and 5) improve the morals of public administration and public life in general.[1] To reach these objectives, Alexandre's government endowed the ULCC with administrative and financial autonomy and jurisdiction over the whole territory of the Republic of Haïti.

Since its founding on September 8, 2004, the ULCC has taken numerous steps with the purpose of abating the prevalence of corruption in Haïti. For instance, most recently, it provided the World Bank's (WB) branch of 'capacity development' —viz. the Institute — with the help that it needed to develop a governance and anti-corruption assessment of Haïti's public administration sector. As a report designed to complement the broad, multi- country studies of the international organizations (e.g., Transparency International) that monitor governmental corruption across the world, this evaluation proved to be somewhat useful. Given the data that it generated, it helped Haïtian leaders —along with members of the international community —to acquire more detailed knowledge with regard to the state of governance in Haïti. Other actions taken by the ULCC have included, but have not been limited to, financial fraud investigations, anti-corruption conferences for politicians, and national awareness events for the public.

Curious about the effects of these measures on Haïti's level of corruption, I will examine the administrations of two of the country's former presidents —namely Jean- Bertrand Aristide and René Préval —to determine the efficacy of the anti-corruption measures undertaken before and after the founding of the ULCC.[2] To arrive at this objective, I will answer the following research question: have the actions taken and the anti-corruption measures adopted by the ULCC succeeded in diminishing the level of corruption that plagues the country's public administration sector?

Fundamentally, this question is very important because it will help to identify some of the factors that have allowed corruption to take over the government of Haïti (GoH). In addition, it is important to note that no one else has conducted an analysis that is parallel to the one proposed herein; that is to say that no other researcher has ever essayed to evaluate the actions of the ULCC. Given the unprecedented nature of this analysis, it warrants completion.

ENDNOTES:

[1] I learned about the objectives of the ULCC from a French version of its charter, which can be found at: http://gerardlatortue.org/bpm/pdf/decrets/ulcc.pdf

[2] Of the multiple terms that these two leaders served, I will only examine Haïti's levels of corruption from Febru-

ary 2001 to February 2004 and from May 2006 to May 2011.

Chapter 3
Literature Review

Before plunging into an analysis of the corrupt practices that dominate the GoH, it is very important to discuss the literature that surrounds the topic of corruption. Throughout the remainder of this section, this work will engage in such a discussion by: 1) succinctly reviewing the theories and debates that have emerged from previous research projects on corruption and 2) assessing the correctness and completeness of this knowledge. Overall, the literature written on the subject of corruption is vast. Despite the voluminous and intricate nature of the body of works written on this topic, the term "corruption" is one that lacks an adequate definition (Peters and Welch, 2001, p. 156).[3] Given the indefinite nature of its meaning, some scholars have refrained from defining it in their analyses (e.g. Gill, 1998). However, others have embraced its common definition —which is the belief that it is fundamentally characterized by the misuse of "the state as a tool for private gain" (Rose- Ackerman, 2008, p. 341). As some scholars have argued (e.g. McGirr, 2011), because this elementary definition fails to reveal the types of actions that constitute 'misuse', it is virtually useless by virtue of its vagueness.

Given the equivocal nature of this frequently encountered definition, several theorists (e.g. Aidt, 2003 and Kurer, 2005) have attempted to define political corruption in a manner that is more precise and sophisticated. Cognizant of the effects that the definition of the term can have on the direction of their analyses, these scholars have offered various redefinitions of the phenomenon.[4] For instance, Leys (1965) has described it as "a standard of behaviour [sic] according to which [an] action...breaks some rule, written or unwritten, about the proper purposes to which a public office or a public institution may be put" (p. 221). Similarly, in line with the legalistic essence of this definition, Nye (1967) has defined political corruption as "behavior which [sic] deviates from the formal duties of a public role because of private-regarding...pecuniary or status gains; or violates rules against the exercise of certain types of private- regarding influence" (p. 419). According to Peters and Welch (2001), although these definitions' reliance on unequivocal, "legalistic criteria" make them somewhat useful, they have two major defects. To begin with, in an oxymoronic way, they are altogether too restrictive and too comprehensive in scope because all unlawful acts are not inevitably corrupt and all corrupt acts are not always lawful (Peters and Welch 2001, p. 156). Secondly, given their dependence on legal guidelines, Peters and Welch (2001) maintain that these descriptions become inadequate when the deeds of an actor deviate from legal norms that do not correspond to specific codes or when the duties of office or the proper rules of influence become blurry (p. 156). Given these significant deficiencies, it is evident that the definition of corruption needs revision and/or development.

Unlike Leys and Nye, Klitgaard (1998) has examined corruption by using a widely accepted framework known as "the principal-agent-client" (PAC) model. According to him and others who have used this scheme, corruption is, in effect, a malfunction of the process within which (P)—the principal (e.g. an elected official) —authorizes A —an intermediary agent (e.g. a functionary) —to provide services or goods to a group of beneficiaries —i.e. the clients (C). Within this model, corruption takes place when the agent (A) forsakes the principal's (P) interest and instead pursues her/his own end by demanding or deliberately collecting a benefit from the recipient of a service or good —the client (C). To describe how corruption operates, Klitgaard (1998) summarizes the phenomenon with equation C=M+D– A, with C being corruption, M standing for monopoly of power, D being discretion by officials, and A signifying accountability. More precisely, according to Klitgaard (1998), the set of circumstances that engenders corruption is one during which there is a lack of accountability between the principal (P) and the agent (A) (p. 24). In line with this assumption, corruption is likely to occur when P orders A to allocate some goods or grant some services and provides her/him with a significant degree of discretion in distributing them.

Overall, Klitgaard's (1998) definition of corruption is very useful because it helps us to better understand the nature of the phenomenon by describing the sets of circumstances under which it occurs. However, like Leys's (1965) and Nye's (1967) definitions, it has its problems. For instance, because the model upon which it is founded (i.e. the PAC model) allegedly regards corruption as "criminal behaviour [sic] by some agents entrusted to act on behalf of a (honest/benevolent) [sic] principal," Rothstein (2011) claims that it is imperfect (p. 230). The flaw of the underlying framework of this definition stems from the fact that it is hard, and sometimes impossible, to determine who such a benevolent principal might be in a system that is totally corrupt (Rothstein, 2011, p. 230). Furthermore, Rothstein (2011) holds that the PAC model suffers from another defect —that is that it is biased in regarding "'the people' [as] the (honest and benevolent) principal and the political leaders [as] the corrupt agents" (p. 230). This bias is problematic because it provides the false sense that only public officials practice corruption.

Dissatisfied with Klitgaard's definition and those of other scholars who have used the PAC model to set forth their interpretation of the phenomenon, Rothstein (2011) —in conjunction with Kurer (2005) and Teorell (2007) —offers a definition that is supposedly more accurate. After dismissing the abovementioned standard definition of political corruption, with the help of his colleagues, Rothstein (2011) offers a definition that purportedly encourages "non-discrimination in the exercise of public authority" (p. 230). He maintains that his definition is more complete and less problematic than the common definition of corruption because "it can be traced back to normative theories about justice as well as democracy" (p. 230). Moreover, he contends that it is particularly useful and practical in light of its reliance on the concept of 'impartiality'. In a political system, although neutrality can certainly impel public officials "to treat people alike irrespective of personal relationships and personal likes and dislike" (Cupit, 2000 as cited in Rothstein, 2011, p. 230), it cannot prevent corruption. As a result, despite its promotion of a juridical model of justice, Rothstein's (2011) definition of corruption is, for an important reason, faulty. Owing to the Aristotelian belief that human beings are by nature political creatures and the argument that impartial moral behavior requires "superhuman powers of thought, superhuman knowledge and no human weaknesses" (Hare, 2011, p. 182), impartiality within a political milieu is non-achievable.

Of the four definitions discussed above, one cannot positively state that either of them is of a higher-quality than the remaining two because, as demonstrated above, all three of them have their limitations. In spite of this fact, the definition that relies on the PAC model will prove to be most useful to this thesis.5 This is because I am primarily concerned with examining the ways in which corruption takes place between public officials and their underlings.

Aside from describing corruption, scholars who examine the practice also focus on its causes. The first, and perhaps the oldest, of the theories that explain the reasons why corruption arises and persists is one that considers corrupt practices to be efficiency- enhancing mechanisms that "grease the wheels" of public bureaucracies. Proponents of this idea argue that corrupt transactions allow private citizens and public servants to bypass the inefficiencies of governmental organizations by: 1) accelerating bureaucratic procedures and 2) introducing competition for government resources with the consequence that goods or services are apportioned more expeditiously than they otherwise would have been. In general, the empirical literature surrounding the validity of this theory is quite extensive. For instance, by using two separate models to analyze the effects of corruption on governmental bureaucracies, Lui (1985), along with Beck and Maher (1986), discovered that bribes can indeed impel government bureaucracies to become more efficient. Similarly, using Ronald Coase's Theorem to examine the effects of bribes on the allocation of government resources, Shleifer and Vishny (1994) show the ways in which bribery may facilitate an efficient allocation of such resources. Despite corruption's ability to make government bureaucracies more efficient, Boycko,

Shleifer, and Vishny (1996) maintain that it is not the best way to allocate government resources.

To further examine the causes of corruption, scholars rely upon the aforementioned PAC model.[6] Scholars (e.g. Klitgaard, 1998) who perceive corruption through this theoretical lens hold that the phenomenon comes into existence when a "benevolent" principal assigns a task to a malevolent intermediary agent to whom s/he provides decision-making power. Given the power that s/he possesses, this agent might exploit her/his position. As a result, whenever a bureaucrat delegates a task to an agent, there is always a potential for corruption (Aidt, 2003). The level of corruption that exists within any establishment is always determined by how well-designed its structure of governance is (p. 635).

Unlike the proponents of the theory above, some scholars argue that all government agents are corruptible. These theorists offer a different view on the PAC model and claim that there is no moral difference between agents and principals. In light of this view, they do not consider principals to be the supposed designers of bureaucratic systems. Consequently, these scholars think that governmental bureaucracies are likely to be very incompetent. In describing the origin of this theory, Aidt (2003) maintains that "this view of government...has a long tradition within public choice...but has recently been advocated forcefully in the context of corruption by Shleifer and Vishny..." (p. 642). Moreover, they have invented the term 'the grabbing hand' to argue that governments are controlled by politicians who "do not maximize social welfare and instead pursue their own selfish objectives" (Shleifer and Vishny, 1998, p. 4). Although these theorists do not think that privatization and deregulation can ultimately defeat corruption, they believe that "smaller government[s] may indeed be cleaner government[s]" (Rose-Ackerman, 2000, p. 99). To criticize these views, some scholars have argued that government intervention does curb corruption (Hopkin and Rodríguez-Pose, 2007). To support their claims, they have pointed to the fact that Scandinavian countries with big governments have 'cleaner' governments than market-oriented countries like the U.S.

In terms of the specific causes of political corruption, the literature cites numerous factors as culprits. To begin with, ancient political philosophers such as Plato and Aristotle argue —respectively in The Republic and Politics and Nicomachean Ethics —that societal inequality in its various forms along with human predisposition toward self-centeredness set forth the circumstances for corruption. According to these philosophers, as an aggressive type of materialistic acquisitiveness, greed (pleonexia in Greek) is a dangerous constituent of the human soul (psuchê in Greek, or anima in Latin) (Balot, 2001). Because of it, some theologians (e.g. Barclay, 1975) hold that human beings always ruthlessly pursue their own interests and seek to acquire the possessions of others with total disregard for human rights. In De Anima, Aristotle explains the source of greed by maintaining that human beings always yearn for more material possessions because they must incessantly strive as creatures with souls that must always be involved in motion. In the same vein, Machiavelli contends that even the most righteous human beings can become corrupted through ambition and greed. He expresses this view best when he writes that "One can make this generalization about men: they are ungrateful, fickle, liars, and deceivers, they shun danger and are greedy for profit..." (*The Prince*).

These philosophical beliefs are as true today as they were during ancient times. For this reason, in their attempt to explain the forces that drive political corruption, modern-day scholars cite a plethora of factors that includes, but is not limited to, politicians' insatiable desires for wealth, the absence of accountability within governmental sectors, peer pressure, and a lack of administrative transparency within bureaucratic systems (Rahman, 1986, Rose-Ackerman, 1999, Treisman, 2000). Although these factors are present within all corrupt governments, in order for corruption to flourish within any government, several preconditions must be present. One of these prerequisites consists of the late or punctual disbursement of low and uneven salaries for public officials with large dependent families. In countries that are politically unstable and impoverished, public servants encounter a lot of financial insecurity. As a result, they feel compelled to behave in a manner that is corrupt by taking advantage of rare opportunities that are financially rewarding to support their immediate and extended families.

To make the point that certain economic milieus are more conducive to corruption than others, some development scholars contend that countries that obtain a large portion of their national income from oil-related commercial activities are frequently more corrupt than those without oil. For instance, Karl (2003) claims that oil-rich countries are often also governed more poorly, possess a culture of rent-seeking, and endure more incidences of civil conflict. In keeping with this assumption, once may surmise that the governments of such countries are more likely to be corrupt because they present their members with more opportunities for personal enrichment. Although Karl's conclusion seems logical, the empirical evidence on the correlation between the presence of economic rents, corruption, and political instability in oil-rich countries is remarkably scarce. According to Arezki and Brückner (2009), the literature written on this subject matter "has been either anecdotal or is plagued by endogeneity biases related to difficult-to-measure (and often unobservable) cross- country differences..." (p. 3). Given the existence of such a flaw within the literature, it is therefore an incautious act to assert that fortunes derived from petroleum directly or indirectly cause corruption.

v\Overall, the literature on the causes of corruption has some significant flaws. For instance, within it, there are not many studies that have ascertained the origin of corruption at the personal level. Although numerous works have identified some of the factors that directly give rise to corrupt practices, corruption is nonetheless a phenomenon that calls for individual choices by particular individuals at certain points of decision and interaction. For this reason, the phenomenon is fundamentally defined by the way in which individuals behave. However, the literature written on the causes of corruption is not very concerned with the particular factors that that cause the phenomenon to beget corrupt societies. In general, scholars have neglected to address personal incentives (e.g. moral values, social statuses, power, and interpersonal dynamics) in their works.

Furthermore, given that they are based on principles that do not apply to all cultures, many of the conclusions that scholars have reached regarding the causes of corruption are very limited. Although no singular factor can be said to be the main cause of corrupt practices, there are several studies in the literature that have identified the general institutional variables that accompany high levels of corruption (McGirr 2011). For instance, (Treisman 2000) and several other scholars have conducted large-n, cross-national studies through which they have measured the phenomenon and identified some variables that correlate with it.[7] Despite the existence of such studies, the discourse on the causes of corruption is still somewhat deficient.

As far as anti-corruption measures, the literature on this topic is currently shaped by a major debate. While some scholars argue that corruption in governance can be controlled through universal techniques, others maintain that the phenomenon is so multi-faceted that scholars need to analyze it in its historical and cultural contexts and, in consequence, must offer particularistic solutions. In their attempt to provide countries with effective anti- corruption measures, scholars on both sides of the debate have written analyses that focus on four different aspects of corruption. These research areas comprise assessments that focus on: systemic corruption; Rule of Law; public administration systems; and the role of nongovernmental organizations. Although the studies devoted to each area share the same objective, the problems that they examine are considerably different.

Scholars who focus on systemic corruption argue that many donor-supported anti- corruption initiatives fail to produce desired results because they do not take into consideration the systemic yet specific nature of corruption. As one of the scholars who take part in the anti-corruption discourse, Johnston (1997) describes systemic corruption as a "situation in which the major institutions and processes of the state are routinely dominated and used by corrupt individuals and groups, and in which many people have few practical alternatives to dealing with corrupt officials" (p. 7). As this quote illustrates, corruption is endemic to a country only when it becomes a necessary and normative element of that country's socio-political and economic systems.

In general, scholars who study systemic corruption attribute its causes to the existence of organizational flaws in states' institutional frameworks and their inability to ensure that their public servants and common citizens adhere to their laws. Upon examining the political systems of corrupt countries, academic analysts of systemic corruption discover that systemically corrupt countries are the ones whose public sectors fall prey to 'state capture' and whose political systems are fundamentally 'neo-patrimonial'.

When the public sectors of corrupt countries succumb to 'state capture', they involuntarily allow private actors (e.g

. business elites and criminal organizations) to manipulate their lawmaking processes in their favor by failing to stop them from secretly rewarding public officials for their political support. On the other hand, countries with neo- patrimonial political systems are states in which politicians hold on to power through personal patronage, rather than through elections and/or ideology. In governments controlled by neo-patrimonialism, the right to rule belongs to individuals and not to the governmental institutions that establish public positions of authority (Bratton, 1994, p. 458). In consequence, in neo-patrimonial political systems, public servants occupy offices in order to aggrandize themselves instead of catering to the necessities of their countries and fellow citizens. In states with either or both of these systems, accession to positions of authority and the preservation of power require a lot of resources. Because politicians often, if not always, profit handsomely from their positions of power, they have almost no interest in implementing anti-corruption measures. For these reasons, levels of corruption in systemically corrupt countries are hard to reduce.

To combat corruption in countries that are systemically corrupt, scholars have offered multiple solutions. For instance, Johnston urges corrupt countries to socially empower their common citizens (p. 3). According to him, although institutional reforms are essential to any anti-corruption strategy, they alone cannot diminish levels of corruption in countries that are systemically corrupt (p. 2). Social empowerment is necessary in such states because it provides the support needed for institutional changes and "help institutionalize reform for the long term by linking it to lasting interests contending in active political and social processes" (abstract).

In the same way, Ozfar (2007) has argued in favor of the establishment of democracy. According to him, democracy has a good chance of reducing the level of corruption in systemically corrupt countries because the elections that take place within democratic systems provide a means for the systematic removal of corrupt regimes from power (p. 261). To support this claim, Ozfar cites the work of Persson and Tabellini (2005) and contends that the literature on corruption reveals a strong inverse relationship between democracy and corruption (p. 261). In addition, Ozfar (2007) urges systemically corrupt countries to change their laws so as to allow common citizens to file civil lawsuits against public officials whenever they neglect their duties or when they mismanage public funds (p. 264). Correspondingly, he also endorses a process called qui tam —a system through which private persons can file criminal charges against public servants for their role in corruption schemes (p. 264). Ozfar thinks that the implementation of these two policies "could lead to a significant improvement in integrity in many systemically corrupt countries where the prosecutor's office has been compromised" (p. 264). His assumption reposes on on the fact that public servants would stop engaging in corrupt behavior in light of their fear of legal prosecution from common citizens and/or other politicians who might want to harm them.

Unlike scholars who study systemic corruption, academic analysts who focus on Rule of Law primarily take stock of matters that strictly pertain to the governance of legal institutions. According to these Rule of Law advocates, the legislators of corrupt countries should enact laws that protect the autonomy of all citizens in the political and economic spheres (Carothers, 2003, p. 8).

Moreover, the judicators in such states should apply the law in a manner that is impartial, uniform, and well-organized (Carothers, 2003, p. 8). Above all, the defenders of Rule of Law measures contend that legal practitioners in corrupt states should unreservedly adopt the design of the legal systems found in Western countries so as to provide independence to the judicial branch of their governments.

To these scholars, the independence of the judiciary is necessary because it "is fundamental to the overall integrity of the rule of law" (de Asis, 2006, p. 4). To proclaim the advantages of Western justice systems, de Asis (2006) cites recent research which, she argues, has found a strong link between judicial independence and economic growth (p. 4). Given the obsession of Rule of Law promoters with Western-style justice systems and their aversion toward traditional systems of justice and even civil law, Carothers (2003) maintains that "their outlook on the Rule of Law can certainly be criticized for its narrowness" (p. 8). What is more, he further criticizes Rule of Law defenders for relying more on their instincts than on well-researched knowledge (p. 9) and for not knowing what the essence of the rule of law is (p. 8).

In terms of preventing corruption, the Rule of Law literature places a lot of emphasis on the capacity-building of justice systems in corrupt countries. The anti-corruption measures that Rule of Law scholars prescribe consist mainly of the enactment of more specialized anti corruption laws and the restructuring of law enforcement agencies. For instance, de Asis (2006) claims that some Rule of Law programs "have recently included training judges, prosecutors and administrative staff in the new domain of international anticorruption, in particular building awareness of the new set of institutions and resources now available to the legal and judicial sector" (p. 10). According to her, Rule of Law reformers also promote another frequent policy that forces the members of the judiciaries of corrupt countries to disclose their personal assets and net worth to their compatriots upon appointment or election and every year thereafter (p. 11). Aside from these capacity-building measures, some scholars claim that most corrupt countries should put in place modern and specialized institutions that have the mandate to deal with complex financial crimes and other complicated problems that pertain to corruption. Although these measures are increasingly becoming part of donor policy frameworks, not many countries are succeeding in using them to curb their levels of corruption. In general, the literature shows poor results from specialized anti-corruption initiatives. In many cases, after reforms took place, politicians failed to follow new laws, codes of conduct, and rules of transparency.

On a different note, the third research area that anti-corruption strategists focus on when examining corruption constitute the public administration systems of developing countries and the reforms through which they could be improved. In the literature on public administration systems, two types of reforms are prominent; they consist of public sector management (PSM) and public finance management (PFM) reforms. As schemes that deal with the production, delivery, and allocation of public goods and services by governments to private citizens, these reforms aim to improve the management of public resources and bring about more transparency in the decision making processes of governmental organizations. What is more, governments use PSM and PFM reforms to increase levels of transparency and accountability within their public sectors. For instance, with sponsorship from the World Bank (WB) and the International Monetary Fund (IMF) and under the influence of the New Public Management (NPM) 'movement' (Development Policy Management Division, 2003, p. xi), many developing countries have, in their attempt to combat corruption, instituted these reforms within the past two decades.

In addition to focusing on the public administration systems of developing countries that are corrupt, anti-corruption scholars also discuss the effects that non-governmental organizations can have on anti-corruption initiatives. While some scholars argue that NGOs can have positive effects on the corruption levels of developing countries, others maintain that countries with poor infrastructures should not depend too much on the services from such organizations. According to scholars who make the latter argument, instead of counting on NGOs, developing countries that are dealing with corruption should strive to improve the ways in which public servants govern their public sectors. As a country that depends on NGOs for more than two-third of the basic needs of its citizens, overreliance on the services provided by NGOs can certainly prove to be a problem in Haïti. For this reason, many public figures have in the recent past argued that NGOs constitute a problem instead of a solution for the impoverished country.

Although development scholars have published a large amount of work on anti- corruption measures, the literature on how to best solve corruption suffers from several flaws. First, many of the works that examine the efficacy of anti-corruption approaches have only focused on what donors have done and the ways in which they have allocated funds. Despite the existence of this bias, the number of studies that in fact possess a partner-country foundation is significantly limited. Another problem with the literature rests with the fact that it fails to comprise many successful anti-corruption cases. Consequently, when attempting to identify which practices work best against the corruption, scholars are left with a few choices. According to Klitgaard (1988), Hong Kong's Independent Commission Against Corruption (ICAC) is among the small number of well-known success stories. Fearing that corruption would negatively affect their ability to govern Hong Kong during its colonial days, British officials created this agency and equipped it with a well-paid and highly-skilled group of bureaucrats. During its years of existence, the ICAC succeeded in keeping levels of corruption low by conducting thorough investigations and by successfully prosecuting numerous corrupt public functionaries and private citizens. Given its achievements, the ICAC certainly has the potential to serve as a model to which administrators can turn when using an enforcement approach to fight corruption. However, given its resemblance to the Weber's Ideal, this model is seriously limited. At present, countries of the developing world cannot successfully duplicate the ICAC's success because they lack the support system (e.g. extensive funding and well-trained professionals) that this agency had when it was in existence.

Overall, given my familiarity with the literature on corruption and Haïti's political culture, I hypothesize that the policies adopted by the ULCC have had little to no effect on the dependent variable of this research project: i.e., Haïti's level of corruption. I hypothesize the ULCC's ability to successfully combat corruption is adversely affected by the following independent variables: a high level of poverty, the existence of a dysfunctional national judicial system, and the lack of transparency within all branches of Haïti's government. Regarding the way in which I will defend the said hypothesis, I plan on using data from reputable non-governmental organizations (NGOs) (e.g. Transparency International and/or the World Bank) to show that Haïti's level of public corruption has hardly changed —and perhaps increased —since the establishment of the ULCC. Though I am cognizant of the fact that numerous critics argue to the contrary, I plan on examining and openly criticizing the missteps of the ULCC during some of the scandals that took place after their founding. More importantly, I will also directly reference the fact that Haïtian law is very outdated and deficient in several areas. Some of the government's current areas of deficiencies include, but are not limited to the following: operation of the judicial system; organization and operation of the executive branch; and customs law enforcement.

ENDNOTES:

[3] Because corruption consists of numerous types of actions, scholars use multiple typologies when they speak of the phenomenon. The most frequent distinctions they make include: 'systemic' versus 'individual' or 'opportunistic' corruption; 'grand' versus 'petty' corruption; 'administrative corruption' versus 'state capture'; and 'centralized' versus 'decentralized' corruption (Huntington, 1968, and Thomas and Meagher, 2004).

[4] Corruption's meaning is important because it affects the direction that scholars follow when conducting their studies on the subject matter. Aidt (2003) puts this best when he writes that "the definition of the concept de-

termines what gets modeled and what empiricists look for in the data."

[5] Overall, among the literature that exists on the meaning of political corruption, not much progress has been made since Heidenheimer (1970) presented his classifications of the definitions of the phenomenon (Werner, 1983, p. 147). According to this scholar, corruption has three types of definitions. The first type constitutes public-office-centered definitions, the second comprises public-interest-centered definitions, and the final type consists of market-centered definitions. To learn more about these types of definition, consult Heidenheimer's (1970) work.

[6] This model inherits its name from the principal–agent problem, which pertains to the various contrarieties that a principal faces when s/he orders an agent to defend her/his interests.

[7] Through several numerical analyses that he conducted for his paper, Treisman (2000) discovered that "Countries with Protestant traditions, histories of British rule, more developed economies, and (probably) higher imports [tend to be] less 'corrupt' than countries that lacked these attributes (p. 399)." Furthermore, he also stumbled upon the fact that countries with federal governments are more likely to be more corrupt than those with different forms of government.

Chapter 4
First Case Study

Political Background

Since the fall of Jean-Claude Duvalier's murderous and kleptocratic regime, Haïti has been the battleground of an incessant struggle for political justice. On one side of this conflict, many politicians have tried to gain control of the country's government in order to enrich themselves and defend the interests of their cohorts. With support from the members of Haïti's upper class, they have sought to establish an "aristocratic democracy" —a pseudo- democratic system of government in which the common people periodically elects the members of an exclusive ruling class to govern. On the other side of this political struggle, the members of Haïti's lower and middle classes have tried to put in place institutions that are committed to the satisfaction of the country's public needs and aspirations (Fatton, 2002, p. 77). By working under the guidance of civil society institutions, these common citizens have tried to bring about a more impartial democracy —one that stands firm against the domination of a select group of politicians or class.

Unwilling to tolerate the self-seeking objectives of Haïti's class of kleptocrats, Jean- Bertrand Aristide —a man who came from humble beginnings —decided to lend his support to the masses. Before becoming Haïti's first democratically elected president, he used his role as a Catholic priest and his renown as an advocate of the poor to fervently speak against many of Haïti's deceitful and bloodthirsty politicians. Drawing on "an interpretation of {the} Christian faith through the poor's suffering...struggle and hope," Aristide argued in favor of "tout moun se moun" —the idea that all Haïtians were equal in their humanity and that Haïti should not be divided across class-based lines (Berryman, 1987).[8] For popularizing this philosophy, which relied upon liberation theology, the Salesian priest paid a steep price. On several occasions, numerous armed bandits tried to assassinate him and his supporters. For instance, "At a service held on August 23{, 1987,}" a lone assassin attempted but failed to killed Aristide after shooting at him from "a mere 20 paces" away, while he "was speaking to a large crowd assembled in an abandoned cannery" (Farmer, 1994). Similarly, on the morning of September 11, 1988, scores of thugs tried to kill him while he was leading a mass at the Saint-Jean Bosco Church in Port-au-Prince. At the end of this violent attack, although Aristide made it out alive, his assailants used knives, machetes, and automatic firearms to kill and injure some of his supporters.

In December of 1990, with support from his National Front for Change and Democracy (Front National pour le Changement et la Démocratie, or FNCD), Aristide took control of Haïti's presidency. In an election that several noteworthy international observers (e.g., U.S. president James E. "Jimmy" Carter, Jr.) claimed was largely fair and nonviolent, he earned almost three-fourth of the people's votes. By defeating Marc Louis Bazin, one of Jean-Claude Duvalier's former Ministers, Aristide became "the messiah who...{had} overcome...the satanic forces of Duvalierism, privilege, and corruption" (Fatton, 2002, p. 78). In spite of his popularity, he faced several serious political obstacles once elected president. Although he adopted practical policies and practiced good governance, his foes wanted him to step down. His efficient control of Haïti's public finances and notable success in fighting financial and violent crimes could not quench his rivals' thirst for power and their hatred toward him and his antibourgeois rhetoric. In the end, the forces that united against Aristide proved to be unstoppable.

Eight months after his inauguration, in September 1991, numerous officers of the Haïtian army (Forces Armées d'Haïti, or Fad'H) joined forces and waged an insurgency against his regime. Under the guidance of Lieutenant General Raoul Cédras and two other persons from Haïti's Army and National Police force, they succeeded in overthrowing his government and forcing him into exile. While living abroad, Aristide managed to maintain his renown among Haïti's masses despite having severed ties with the party that allowed him to ascend to power —the FNCD.[9] Furthermore, he sought and received the support of many in the international community by tilting public opinion against the junta that had deposed him. More than three years after his forced departure, with military support from the William J. "Bill" Clinton government, he returned to Haïti to serve the remainder of his term in office.

After completing his first presidential term, Aristide claimed to have withdrawn from Haïti's political life (Hallward, 2007). Despite this supposed retirement, he helped form a political unit several weeks after his first term came to an end. Shortly after its founding, this institution —which emerged out of an anti-Duvalierist and populist movement that formally began in 1990 —had become a fully functional party, one named the Lavalas Family (Fanmi Lavalas, or FL). Not only had this party's leaders written a constitution that defined the contours of its structure of leadership, they had formulated a program

—one which contained numerous proposals that relied on suggestions obtained from a diverse group of experts (Hallward, 2007). In describing this program's quality, Aristide claimed that it was so well- crafted that the World Bank held it in high esteem. According to him, the World Bank's endorsement came from the intergovernmental institution's recognition of the proposal as a "genuine program {and} a coherent plan for the transformation of {Haïti} and not as "a bundle of empty promises" (Hallward, 2007). Overall, given the FL's possession of such an exceptional platform of reforms, it became the entity that would help Aristide to get reelected.

Five years after becoming president, Aristide once again took control of Haïti's presidency. On February 7, 2001, thousands of Haïtians attended his formal induction into office in Haïti's capital, the city of Port-au-Prince. Worryingly, his inauguration ceremony followed a series of scandalous elections that took place during May 21, July 9, and November 26 of the year 2000. In the May 21 and July 9 elections, Aristide's left-of-center party, the Lavalas Family, fared extremely well on three fronts. First, it obtained the majority of seats available in both houses of Haïti's parliament by winning 18 of the 19 seats contested in the Senate and 72 of the 83 seats in the Chamber of Deputies (Inter- Parliamentary Union, 2000). Second, it received more than three-fourth of the votes for mayors and took most seats in urban and rural district assemblies —which consisted of municipal boards and boards of administration of communal sections (Conseils d'Administration des Sections Communales, or CASECs) (Inter-Parliamentary Union, 2000). Third, during the presidential election of November 26, 2000, Aristide obtained almost 92% of the people's votes to become the leader of Haïti's semi-presidential system of government (Cameron, 2007, p. 419). By winning elections by such wide margins, Aristide and his party faced a major problem.

Because their victories seemed "too good to be true", Aristide and the Lavalas Family's rule became almost illegitimate. Given their feelings of doubt, the political adversaries of the FL, as members of various opposition parties —started to plan a coup against Aristide as he assumed the presidency. Furthermore, given the accusations of electoral fraud, Aristide faced pressure from the United States, other foreign powers, and international organizations. For instance, after the Organization of American States (OAS) raised objections against the Provisional Electoral Council's (Conseil Electoral Provisoire, or CEP) calculations for the senatorial seats, President Bill Clinton's administration put a stop to Haïti's reception of aid from the U.S. government

(Farmer, Smith, and Nevil, 2003). "In April 2001, after cutting off its own aid to Haïti's government, the U.S. blocked the release of $145 million in previously agreed loans from the Inter-American Development Bank {IDB}, and of another $470 million scheduled for the following years" (Hallward, 2004). Similarly, the European Union (EU) "decided to block $49 million in aid," while suspending the "$17.7m intended to help cover the country's budget deficit" (BBC News, 2001). Aside from the aid embargo, Aristide's image as an honest leader and advocate of the poor lost its luster in light of the accusations leveled against his party and regime. As a result, before the start of his second term, his popularity among the masses declined.

To determine the level of corruption within Aristide's government, this segment of the thesis will explore two different scandals. First, it will discuss in greater depth the elections that took place right before Aristide's second entrance into office. Second, it will examine his alleged involvement in a national pyramid scheme through which Haïti's uneducated poor —in conjunction with members of the middle class —lost tens of millions of U.S. dollars (USD). Thereafter, it will call attention to several reports through which numerous public officials have accused Aristide of embezzlement and money-laundering. In all three of these explorations, this unit will primarily focus on the functions of Haïti's governmental institutions and will address the steps that these agencies took to deal with matters that pertain to political corruption. This emphasis is critical because it will help to uncover some of the strengths and weaknesses of Haïti's governmental bureaucracies. More specifically, it will allow this section to meet its central aim —which is to determine the efficacy of the anti-corruption measures undertaken before the founding of the ULCC, Haïti's primary anti-corruption agency. Finally, in keeping with what this thesis claimed in its introductory section —i.e., that it plans on using information from Transparency International (TI) —this case study will rely on TI's Corruption Perception Index (CPI) to show the perceived level of corruption that existed in Haïti before the founding of the ULCC.[10]

The First Presidency of René Préval

To gain a comprehensive understanding of the controversy that surrounded the elections of the year 2000, one must revisit the period that followed the end of Aristide's first term in office. On February 7, 1996, after completing his first presidential term, Aristide handed his power over to a candidate who had received a substantive majority of the popular vote —an agronomist named René Garcia Préval. From the day he entered into office, Préval faced several major problems. Fearful of a bloody coup, he stated in his inaugural speech that his "first concern {was} to restore the power of the State" in Haïti (Haïti Progrès, 1996). To this end, he asked the leader of the UN troops who had restored Aristide's rule to stay in Haïti for a longer period of time than anticipated, until law and order prevailed. Because he presented the UN with such an unpopular request, his support among the masses declined drastically. Worse, Préval also faced opposition from members of his own party who were unhappy with his choice of a Prime Minister and with his economic initiatives. Given these obstacles, it is safe to argue that Préval had a very bad start during his first term in office.

As Préval's regime matured, the resignation of his Prime Minister and the disputes that took place over the results of the 1997 legislative elections further compromised its stability. To express their discontent, Préval's adversaries chose to stay out of the second round of voting, insisting that the elections were fraudulent. Unable to strike a deal with his rivals and facing a divided National Assembly, Préval dismissed both legislative houses of Haïti's parliament. In January 1999, he proclaimed that the term of the National Assembly had run out and that he would thus govern Haïti by decree (New York Times, 1999). As Préval neared the end of his presidency, the legislative, municipal, and presidential races of the year 2000 were fast approaching. Furthermore, the country plunged into political disarray as it faced an aid embargo from the U .S. and Canada and as many people lost their lives to politically-motivated acts of violence. Given their seemingly fixed results, these elections heightened the political crisis that began to brew years earlier.

Scandal 1: The Elections of May and July 2000

These elections took place between the members of Jean-Bertrand Aristide's Lavalas Family and a multiparty opposition alliance named the Democratic Convergence (Convergence Démoccratique, or CD). Whereas the FL consisted of one party, the CD contained more than dozen political entities that received support from the members of Haïti's upper class and the U.S. government and consisted of "right-wing evangelicals, business leaders and ex-Duvalierists" (Hallward, 2004). Nonetheless, when Election Day arrived on May 21 and July 9, 2000, members of the Lavalas Family won a decisive victory. As discussed above, the number of votes that they received was so large that it evoked a lot of suspicion. Although there were serious logistical problems, the elections were largely free of violence. What is more, while the ones that took place on May 21 benefited from a high participation rate of more than 60% of the eligible population, the ones of July 9 had a participation rate of roughly 30% (Fatton, 2002). For this reason, officials from the OAS and the Center for International Policy declared these elections to be "a great success for the Haitian population" and maintained that they were Haiti's best in years (Fatton, 2002). However, soon after claiming that these elections were fair, these international monitors retracted their statements when they discovered that the vote counters totaled the votes in an unconstitutional fashion (Morrell, 2000). After all, it seemed that the FL's true colors had shown. Many adversaries alleged that, with the aid of Préval's government, the FL and its supporters tried to bring them to shame. James Morrell (2000) articulates this allegation best when he writes that because Aristide was not "content with merely winning, {he} had his supporters on the electoral commission rig the count in order to deliver first round victories to all nineteen senatorial candidates, of whom eighteen belong to his...party." This purported conspiracy to commit fraud, if true, was not only immoral but also violated Haïti's 1987 Constitution —the latest of the twenty-three constitutions that the country's politicians have passed into law since 1801.

On Questioning the Validity of the Electoral Fraud Allegations Brought against the Lavalas Family

Although some might dismiss the CD's fraud allegations by calling into question its unwavering pursuit of power, it is somewhat harder to disregard the claims of Leon Manus – –the man who served as the leader of the CEP when the elections took place. On December 27, 2000, in a letter to former U.S. Secretary of State Colin L. Powell, Manus denounces Préval and Aristide not only for "violat{ing} all the agreements on democratization with the parties, civil society, and the international community," but also for urging him to publish the results of the May 21 elections against his will (Isidor, 2001). To describe the extent of the fraud that took place after the elections, Manus writes:

> Overall, the night of the elections was one of fraud, with the goal of ensuring the absolute success of the Fanmi Lavalas party. I was summoned to the National Palace, where both President Préval and former President Aristide threatened me with death if I did not publish the manipulated results. I refused to commit such infamy against the Haitian people, and with the support of the international community, I was

> taken out of Haiti and into exile in the United States. At age 76, I'm learning of the difficult conditions of exile. Subsequent to my departure, Presidents Préval and Aristide published the bogus results, which do not reflect the will of the Haitian people. My deepest concern is that Haiti once again has become a one-party de facto dictatorship. (Isidor, 2001).

Given their seriousness, these accusations seem to confirm the guilt of Préval, Aristide, and the FL. However, some Haïtians at the time who supported the FL's victory called into question Manus's credibility by stating that he decided not to endorse the results of the elections in order to comply with the political objectives and desires of the U.S. government. Although these accusations might be true, they have not been substantiated.

On a relevant note, it is also more difficult to repudiate the accusations that the OAS had made against the Lavalas Family. Most notably, it claimed that "major irregularities following the closure of the polls seriously compromised the integrity and credibility of the election" (OAS, 2001). This conclusion rests on three important facts. First, hours after the elections occurred, several unidentified persons stole many of the ballot boxes and replaced them with boxes that contained votes that favored the FL candidates (Isidor, 2001). Second, 2) some vote-tally sheets were mishandled after vote counters had discarded them; and 3) the arrest and subsequent release of numerous opposition candidates (Fatton, 2002). Although these anomalies may have affected the results of some local and municipal elections, the OAS established that most of the offices sought after at those levels were unaffected (OAS, 2001).

However, the most disturbing and uncorrected anomalies that affected the results of the races pertained to the members of the parliament —most conspicuously the members of the Senate. Although the OAS accepted the results of the elections that the CEP organized for the Chamber of Deputies, the organization unreservedly rejected the results of the senatorial races. It claimed to have done so because the CEP used a vote counting method that was deceiving. In order to become a member of Haïti's Senate, as per the provisions of Haïti's 1987 Constitution, a candidate must obtain an absolute majority of the valid votes casted so as to avoid taking part in a second round. After its investigation, the OAS found that the CEP used an unauthorized vote counting method that only took into consideration the ballots casted for the four frontrunners only, therefore providing the winner with a majority in the first round so as to avoid the need to go to a second contest. James Morrell explains this practice best when he writes that the CEP rigged the elections by:

> stopping the counting of senatorial votes at the first four top contenders, thereby contracting the field by a quarter to a third and bumping up the percentages of the front-runners so they could claim an outright majority. By cutting off the count there they unapologetically discarded some 1.1 to 1.2 million votes cast for opposition candidates -- between 25 to 35 percent of the total. (Morrell, 2000).

If the CEP had not used this method, only about half of the 18 FL candidates would have won an absolute majority in the first round as they did. To defend against this allegation, supporters of the FL maintained that the OAS's claims were based on technicalities that were so trivial that they would not have made a difference in the outcomes of the elections. In addition, they have directly referred to the inconsistent nature of the AOS's aforementioned conclusions —which is its rejection of its claim that the elections went well at first.

A Sample of the Results of the Senate Races of the May 21 Elections[11]

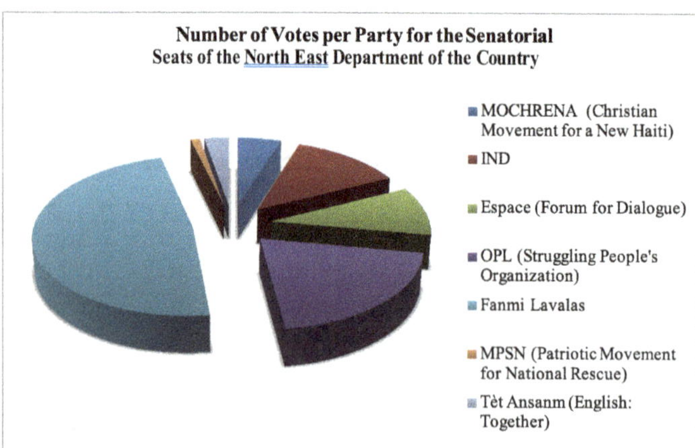

* N.B.: The chart above is strictly based on the disputed calculations made by the CEP. Also, according to the source from which I obtained the set of data, the results of the senatorial elections for the North East department of Haïti very much resembled that of the elections that occurred elsewhere.

Outraged by the CEP's willingness to hand the Lavas Family a quasi-absolute control of Haïti's government, the CD's leaders decided to take action. To make things right, they presented the FL with option zéro: "the resignation of René Préval...the annulment of the legislative {and Presidential}elections{:} the installation of a new and impartial electoral council," and the unwillingness to allow Aristide to take part in subsequent elections (Fatton, 2002). Aware of the FL's unwillingness to relinquish its political power, the CD tried to denigrate the FL by accusing its leaders of being dictatorial, bloodthirsty, and immoral.

Having reached deadlock over the validity of the results of the May elections, both parties agreed to reconcile their differences through meetings sponsored by the OAS. With the objective of identifying "options and recommendations for resolving...difficulties such as those that have arisen from differing interpretations of the Electoral Law," the OAS met with representatives (e.g., Préval, Aristide, Gerard Pierre-Charles, and Evans Paul) from both parties on multiple occasions (OAS, 2000). Despite taking part in lengthy discussions, both sides ultimately made no major compromises. Although the members of the CD changed some of their party's demands, they remained adamant about certain provisions that the FL found to be preposterous. In consequence, the CD and the FL never reached an agreement.

With the cessation of the OAS-sponsored negotiations and the approaching presidential election of Aristide, the chasm between the FL and its adversaries widened. As the members of the CD continued to dispute the results of the elections, the level of political instability in the country sharply increased. Shortly after the elections, many people protested while others committed countless acts of violence. Furthermore, the newly elected parliament was suddenly "faced with skyrocketing food and gas prices {and} a collapsing currency" (Haïti Progrès, 2000). Despite the existence of these trying obstacles, the newly elected parliamentarians took some significant leadership initiatives. For instance, "Immediately after being sworn in, the legislators...form{ed} committees and working groups. Yvon Neptune, an FL senator for the West Department, was elected as president of the Senate. Extending an olive branch to the opposition, the Lavalas deputies voted in as president of the lower house...a former Duvalierist deputy. " (Haïti Progrès,

2000). Overall, despite these new steps, Haïti's poor continued to suffer as the U.S. and the members of the EU decided to punish its leaders through foreign aid suspension.

Scandal 2: The Pyramid Scheme

In February of 2001, two weeks after his inauguration as President, Aristide proposed and persuaded the legislative branch of Haïti's government to pass a law against the laundering of proceeds earned through the trafficking of illicit drugs and other types of criminal ventures. With the aim of tightening the government's controls on the country's financial sector, the authors of this piece of legislation took into account a set of five different considerations:

- 1st. that the illicit traffic of narcotics and other psychoactive substances —as well as money laundering transactions that are part of increasingly complicated, domestic and international criminal schemes —requires the strengthening of existing sanctions and adoption of new measures;

- 2nd. that such activities generate significant economic returns that invade, infect, and corrupt national institutions and give rise to negative effects on Haïtian society's economic, cultural, and political foundations;

- 3rd. that the laundering of assets derived from illicit drug trafficking constitutes an offense that is detrimental to the country's public order, social peace, and national economy;

- 4th. that in order to preserve the integrity of the country and the reliable nature of its financial system, it is incumbent upon the Haïtian government to prevent and put an end to the laundering of proceeds from criminal activities through appropriate and rigorous measures;

- 5th. that to achieve this end, the struggle of the Haïtian government against money laundering cannot be fought properly without international cooperation and support from financial institutions and monetary agencies. (International Money Laundering Information Network, n.d.).[12]

After its enactment, this law went into effect on April 5, 2001 and promptly led to the establishment of an investigative body called the Central Financial Enquiry Unit (Unité Centrale de Renseignements Financiers, or UCREF). Monitored by Haïti's Ministry of Justice and Public Safety —as well as the National Committee for the Fight against Money Laundering (Comité National de Lutte contre le Blanchiment des Avoirs, or CNLBA)—the UCREF's primary objective was to publish reports and investigate complaints filed by private citizens and/or organizations on matters that pertain to corruption and/or money laundering.

Less than six months after the Haïtian government founded the UCREF, President Aristide began an information campaign during which he used TV and radio advertisements to urge all Haïtians to place their savings in government-backed cooperative banking institutions (Coopératives d'épargne et de credit, or CEC). To entice a large number of people to join this popular movement, these financial institutions offered monthly rates of return that were as high as fifteen percent and "competed for customers by offering cellphones and compact disk players to new depositors and an upfront payout of three months {sic} interest" (Gonzalez, 2002). Unable to resist such propositions, a large number of Haïtians who lived in Haïti and abroad sold their assets and deposited the proceeds in their CEC accounts. To describe the madness that surrounded the CEC scheme, David Gonzalez, of the New York Times, writes the following: "Intoxicated by the promise of easy money, thousands of Haïtians here and abroad sold their cars, mortgaged their homes and emptied their savings accounts...to invest in cooperatives that promised astonishing monthly returns of 10 percent" (Gonzalez, 2002). To support this claim, while living in Haïti as a child at the time, I remember hearing many people claiming that they were so excited about the future returns of their deposits that they abandoned their jobs or stopped going to school.

For months, although many economists and bankers told government officials that these financial institutions were fraudulent, no steps were taking to regulate their activities. For weeks, these institutions recruited more members as they continued to operate without any oversight. Given their continued existence, more and more Haïtians kept selling whatever belongings they had hoping to receive high returns. Nonetheless, as time went by, some people became concerned and warned others that the CECs' offers were too good to be true. However, as President Aristide continued to announce his support for these institutions, many cast their doubts away. Instead of siding with critics, they chose to believe the President's claim that the CECs would help the country to get on the path of rapid economic development.

Despite President Aristide's reassurance to the Haïtian people that the CECs were legitimate businesses, a scandal erupted during the end of the summer of 2002. By that time, almost all of the CECs had declared bankruptcy. As a result, "More than $200 million {had} been lost...{as CEC leaders} took their investors' money and bought luxurious properties, fleets of buses or just spirited it abroad" (Gonzalez, 2002). When the Haïtian people learned about the shutting down of the CECs, many of them became infuriated and decided to take the law into their own hands by burning or looting some of the buildings where the CECs were located. Overall, because a large number of people had lost a lot of money, Haïti became very politically unstable. "With thousands of other people having lost their homes or savings and unsure how they will pay their rent or send their children to school in September," the streets of many cities across Haïti fell victim to chaos (Gonzalez, 2002). Many victimized citizens joined forces and held protests in front of the National Palace and outside the U.S. Embassy in Port-au-Prince.

Many of the protesters held signs that indicated that they wanted the U.S. government to oust Aristide because they felt that, as a former supporter of the CECs, he was behind the fraud that occurred. Living in Haïti at the time, I heard many people say that he had to have known about the scheme because of his ties to some of the leaders of the CECs. For this reason, "Old, idealistic, Lafanmi Lavalas {Lavalas Family} supporters denounced the scandal and ceased to support an Aristide presidency that now amounted to a form of organized crime..." (Girard, 2010). In addition, many grew furious after the leaders of one of the CECs stated via radio that the Aristide government had taken much of their institution's capital to pay the chimè {gang members} and zenglendou {outlaws} affiliated with the government (Deibert, 2005). One of the victims of the CECs' fraudulent schemes spoke with me recently via Facebook and stated the following: "My parents sold their cattle and everything else that they had to invest their money with the co-operatives. Upon learning that we were scammed, we wanted Aristide to die and prayed that God would strike him dead" (F. Cédric, personal communication, December 19, 2011). Overall, aware of the fact that the Haïtian people were rapidly turning against him, Aristide promised on multiple occasions to pay all of the victims back. In the end, despite his claims, no one ever received any money back while he was in office.

However, several months after he involuntarily departed, some of the victims recovered part of their deposits in the form of a small payment. On March 22, 2005, after acknowledging that Aristide directly contributed to the failure of the CECs, Gérard Latortue —the head of Boniface Alexandre's provisional government —established a national reparations bureau for the vic-

VJLS Computer Service & Accessories, KDO S.A., and Se Pa'n Provisions Alimentaires) to help him launder millions of Gourdes and U.S. Dollars (UCREF). More- ıver, the UCREF also found evidence ıat the Republic of China had sent a half illion USD to Aristide's government in :tober of 2001 for the construction of ıniversity called the Aristide Founda- ı University. Although the FAD built physical grounds for this university, e journalists (e.g., Valéry Numa) ar- that Aristide might have used some ıis money to finance his personal 'es (Brown, 2005).

lation to the second scandal dis- ɛd above, the UCREF discovered ɔne of the CECs played a some- important role in the FAD's mon- ndering scheme. Named the Con- · Cooperative of the Shining Sun ɗ'Oie (Coopérative de Consomma- ·leil Brillant Fond'Oie, or COCSOB- is firm maintained control of two

tims. This organization bore the name of Bureau national de réparation des sociétaires victims, or BNRSV. In founding this agency, he announced that "The government...{would} make every effort to compensate the victims within a short period of time" (Radio Métropole, 2005). Several months later, on August 16, the BNRSV paid 2 million Gourdes to the victims who lived in Port-au-Prince and some of the provincial cities (e.g., Jacmel and Gonaïves). Overall, although this agency declared that it would distribute 6 million more Gourdes to the victims, it must be noted that such a sum of money was too small to have really satisfied those who collectively lost numerous millions of USDs to the CECs. Although Alexandre's provisional government should be given credit for trying, its efforts were unsuccessful in repairing the damage that Aristide had allegedly caused in the lives of those who had placed their savings in the hands of the leaders of the CECs.

Anti-Corruption Efforts

As stated toward the end of my literature review, in order to determine if the ULCC had an effect on Haïti's level of corruption, it is my aim to discover if the country's governments handled cases of corruption in an effective manner before the organization's founding. Thus, in this section, to provide my readers with a comparative baseline, I document the steps that the country's government to investigate and/or prosecute Aristide for some of the fraudulent actions discussed in scandal one and two above.

In November of 2004, shortly after the U.S. removed Aristide from power, a judge from the civil tribunal of Port-au-Prince ordered the UCREF —the Central Financial Enquiry Unit that Aristide had ironically created during his second presidency —to investigate the

financial activities of the former p
dent's Foundation for Democracy
dation Aristide pour la Démo
or FAD). On October 15, 1996
tide founded this non-profit orga
"with a simple principle in m
promise of democracy can on
filled if all sectors of Haitian s
able to actively participate in t
ratic life of the nation" (Aristi
tion for Democracy, n.d.). Th
vestigation, the UCREF disc
this organization not only
taxes for a number of yea
rected a complicated mor
scheme.

According to the UCREF,
and with the help of mu
coconspirators (e.g., fo
ter Yvon Neptune, forr
Interior Henry-Claud
mer Senator Myrlan
Aristide opened 17
created multiple sh

bank accounts that its executives had opened at Haïti's Popular Bank (Banque Populaire Haïtienne, or BPH). By publishing a series of charts, the UCREF demonstrated in its investigative report that this CEC had helped to transfer funds from the FAD to some of the shell companies mentioned above. In June of 2004, after it became aware of these connections, the UCREF obtained permission from a judge to freeze the BPH accounts of the COCSOBFO. To show the links that existed between the FAD, COCSOBFO, and some of the aforesaid shell companies, the UCREF created the following chart:

La carte de renseignements suivante met en relief les connections entre les différentes organisations impliquées dans cette criminalité financière organisée.

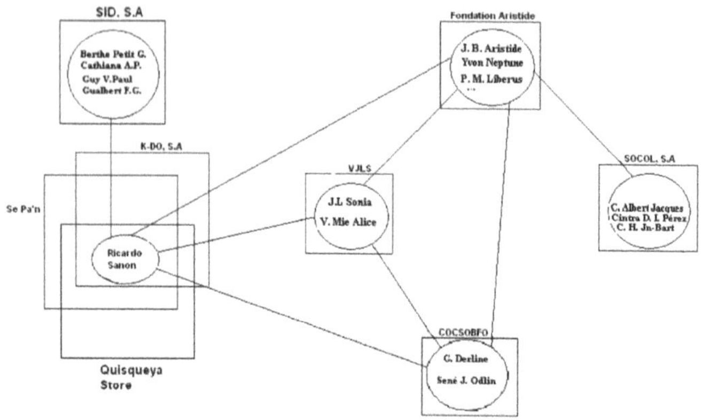

Figure 2.- CARTE DE RENSEIGNEMENTS

Translation of the text above: The following information map demonstrates the connections between the different organizations implicated in this scheme of organized financial crime.

As this diagram shows, the FAD's money laundering scheme was fairly intricate and broad. Given all of the irrefutable evidence that it encountered, at the end of its investigation, the UCREF suggested that the aforesaid persons be brought before justice on money laundering charges. However, despite this recommendation, no courts took serious judicial actions against any of the law-breakers.

Months after it conducted the UCREF investigations, on March 2, 2005, the GoH — in conjunction with a publically-owned telephone company named Telecommunications d'Haïti, S.A.M. (hereinafter referred to as "Teleco") —filed a civil action lawsuit against Aristide and eight other accomplices in the U.S. District Court for the Southern District of Florida. In their complaint, Teleco and the government maintained that Aristide misused his authority to impoverish the Haïtian public. By putting in place a series of intricate money laundering schemes, they contended that he aimed to: "(a) loot the public treasury and launder the illicit proceeds; (b) divert and steal revenues rightfully belonging to the Haitian national telephone company: and (e) encourage, protect, participate and profit from illegal drug trafficking in and through Haiti" (The Republic of Haiti and

Teleco v. Aristide et al., 2005). Aside from accusing him of embezzling Haïti's public funds, they also argued that he trafficked drugs and took part in various other types of criminal activities (e.g., bribery and racketeering). According to them, Aristide not only "diverted to the benefit of himself and others revenues rightfully belonging to plaintiff Teleco," but also "provided safe passage for transshipments of illegal drugs to the U.S." in exchange for bribes. Because of Aristide's involvement in drug trafficking, they claimed that "by 2004 some 20 percent of the cocaine entering the U.S. came through Haiti —a fourfold increase during {his} rule." Overall, given the evidence they presented in their complaint and the findings of the UCREF, it seems likely that Aristide's administration was after all not the high-minded regime that it purported to be.

To bolster the credibility of some of the claims that Teleco and the GoH made in their complaint, it must be noted that several U.S. courts convicted some of the former members of Aristide's administration for their participation in narcotrafficking schemes. For instance, J. Weaver and J. Charles, of the Miami Herald, write that "a federal grand jury probe in Miami has led to 22 convictions of mostly Haitian drug traffickers, ex-police officers and a high-ranking politician close to Aristide" (Charles and Weaver, 2006). Some of the traffickers convicted in U.S. courts included Aristide's former head of security —namely Mr. Oriel Jean. According to a report published by the Dominion, Canadian immigration officers arrested Jean in Toronto in March of 2004 and extradited him to the U.S. to face charges of drug trafficking (Barry-Shaw, 2007). After agreeing to cooperate with the U.S.'s Drug Enforcement Agency, he entered into a plea bargain deal that allowed him to serve less than three years in prison. On a similar note, in February 25, 2004, a notorious trafficker named Beaudoin "Jacques" Ketant told a judge in a Miami courtroom that he had obtained help from Aristide in moving more than forty tons of cocaine between Colombia and the U.S. over a ten-year period —from 1986 to 1996. Before being sentenced to twenty-seven years in prison and ordered to pay a fine of USD 30 million, Ketant told U.S. District Judge Federico A. Moreno that Aristide was a drug kingpin who "controlled the drug trade in Haiti" (Lebowitz, 2004). Ira Kurzban —acting as Aristide's attorney —countered Ketant's claims by stating that his allegations amount to nothing more than "another piece of the effort to politically assassinate" Aristide. Although Ketant —as the godfather of one of Aristide's daughters —had close ties to the former president, it is hard to assess the verity of his statements.

Recently, almost eight years after his conviction, several U.S. news agencies reported that an assistant U.S. attorney wanted a U.S. court to reduce Ketant's sentence to thirteen and a half years. According to this attorney, the U.S. government should reduce Ketant's sentence because "his cooperation led to successful prosecutions of five high-ranking Haitian officials under former President Jean-Bertrand Aristide, including the Port-au-Prince police chief and the security chief at the capital city's airport" (Anderson, 2012). After hearing the assistant attorney's plea, the judge who had convicted Ketant — Chief U.S. District Judge Federico Moreno —did not make an immediate decision and conveyed the concerns that he had regarding Ketant's assets in Haïti and his alleged involvement in a 1997-murder.

Of the civil action lawsuit filed by the GoH against Aristide, it must be noted that — as in the aforesaid criminal cases —the U.S. government succeeded in punishing some of Aristide's partners in crime. In 2011, after a two-and-a-half-week trial and five hours of deliberation, a federal jury convicted Joel Esquenazi and Carlos Rodriguez of multiple money laundering counts for paying more than USD 890,000 in bribes to several of Teleco's officials —e.g. , Robert Antoine, Jean Rene Duperval, and Patrick Joseph (U.S. Department of Justice, 2011). As the former president and executive vice president (in illo ordine) of a profitable telecommunications enterprise named Terra Telecommunications Corp., Esquenazi and Carlos Rodriguez received a harsh sentence for violating the Foreign Corrupt Practices Act of 1977 (FCPA). Together, they received a total of twenty-two years of prison time after they tested their innocence and exercised their constitutional right to a trial. In general, this case seems to have emerged from the complaint that Teleco and the GoH had filed against Aristide and his accomplices in

2005. In its complaint, Teleco relied on a series of financial charts to claim that Aristide had deprived it of some of its revenue by putting in place a system that allowed him to receive kickbacks from multiple U.S.-based telecommunications companies (e.g. Terra Telecommunications Corp., IDT Corporation, and Skytel, Ltd.).

Given the actions that it took against its own nationals and the citizens of Haïti, it is evident the U.S. government strongly opposes corruption and other types of criminal activities (e.g., narcotrafficking). While commenting on the outcome of the Department of Justice's case against Esquenazi and Rodriguez, Assistant Attorney General Lanny A. Breuer stated that the verdict rendered "is another powerful example that bribery of government officials – whether at home or abroad – has serious consequences. In finding the defendants guilty on all charged counts, the jury sent an unmistakable message that paying off foreign officials does not, in fact, pay off" (Department of Justice, 2011). Although this seems true, one must wonder why the U.S. government has chosen to not pursue legal action(s) against Aristide for the role that he played in many of the crimes and schemes discussed above. Although Aristide's lawyers have claimed that many of the accusations made against him are politically-motivated, there are instances where evidence suggests the contrary. For instance, in the report written by officials from the UCREF, Aristide's guilt is substantiated by evidence that seems irrefutable (e.g., checks). Similarly, Ketant's claim that Aristide once controlled much of Haïti's drug trade sounds believable. As someone who once shared close ties to the president, it seems unlikely that he would fabricate accusations out of thin air. The same could be said about the accusations made by several of Aristide's former accomplices. Undoubtedly, although observers have a right to be skeptical, it is nonetheless the duty of foreign governments (e.g. the U.S.) to assess the accuracy of some of these claims given the threat that they pose to their national security and efforts to fight crime.

ENDNOTES:

[8] Phillip Berryman defines liberation theology as "an interpretation of Christian faith through the poor's suffering, their struggle and hope, and a critique of society and the Catholic faith and Christianity through the eyes of the poor" (Berryman, 1987).

[9] After he left the FNCD, Aristide cofounded a new party named the Lavalas Political Organization (Organization Politique Lavalas, or OPL).

[10] Because its CPI "is based on rankings...calculated using a changing set of source surveys," TI has stated that it "is therefore not the appropriate tool for comparisons over time" {italics added} (Transparency International, 2010). Although this is true, it must be noted that the information extracted from the Index is still useful because it temporally correlates with the perception(s) that the Haïtian people and international community hold toward the level of corruption in Haïti.

[11] This chart is my own creation. I made it using data from Morrell's "Haïti Elections" (2000).

[12] The translation of these considerations is mine.

Chapter 5

Second Case Study

The Government of Alexandre and Latortue

Three years after his presidential inauguration, Aristide faced an insurmountable obstacle. Although he tried to incorporate members of the CD into his cabinet, he could not placate nor satisfy the desires of his adversaries. As a result, as time went on, many progressively challenged his authority as Haïti's President. Instead of becoming fonder of his leadership, they remained malcontents and came to see him "as an evil force capable of committing any crime to stay in power" (Fatton, 2002, p. 180). Therefore, in February of 2004, as protesters and armed rebels terrorized Haïti's people, Aristide appeared before the international community and asked for help that would allow him to keep the country under his control. To give urgency to his call, he claimed that thousands of Haïtians would fall victim to senseless acts of violence and that many could flee the country by boat (Cable News Network, 2004). In the end, despite his request for help, Aristide was left with no choice but to relinquish the presidency. On February 29, 2004, he left Haïti with his family and bodyguards on a U.S.-dispatched airplane after receiving pressure from foreign governments —most notably the Bush Administration.

Hours after Aristide's departure, as the next person in the presidential line of succession, Boniface Alexandre became Haïti's interim leader. However, despite being known as a fair-minded and honest person, Haïti's 1987 Constitution required that he relinquish the presidency months after assuming office. According to Article 149 of this document, "Should the office of the President of the Republic become vacant for any reason... .The election of a new President for a new five (5) year term shall be held at least forty-five (45) and no more than ninety (90) days after the vacancy occurs..." (The 1987 Constitution of Haïti, art. 149). Furthermore, in keeping with this Article, Alexandre had to be "invested temporarily with the duties of the President of the Republic by the National Assembly duly convened by the Prime Minister." However, because the terms of most members of parliament had expired under Aristide, this was not possible.

Despite his failure to be confirmed by Haïti's parliament, Alexandre succeeded in taking control of the presidency. As Haïti's new president, in a fifteen speech delivered on February 29, 2004, he stated that his "task w[ould] not be an easy one" and that "No one should take justice into their [sic] own hands" (Epatko, 2004). Shortly after his inauguration as President, an "American-backed council of 'eminent Haitians'" —which consisted of one delegate each of the international community, Lavalas Family, and civil opposition — selected Gérard Latortue to be Haïti's Prime Minister (Polgreen, 2004). After being sworn on March 12, 2004, Latortue, a respected sixty-nine-year-old lawyer and former UN and governmental official, picked only politicians who had no strong party affiliations to become part of his cabinet (Dodds, 2009). To explain his choice of assisting ministers, Latortue stated that his decision was "a way of showing that it is possible to govern this country differently" and that his administration was nonpartisan. Overall, given his political savvy, considerable acquaintance with Haïti's politics, and international work experience, many intellectuals —inside and outside of Haïti —initially saw Latortue as a competent politician.

Shortly after the creation of Haïti's interim government, to help restore order in Port- au-Prince and elsewhere around the country, the UN took an important step. In responding to a request that President Alexandre had submitted to its Security Council, it unanimously passed a resolution that sanctioned the immediate deployment of an international military force. Consisting of U. S., French, and Canadian military and law enforcement personnel, this Multinational Interim Force (MIF) had to carry out a multifaceted mission. Within three months, it had to: 1) help with the delivery of humanitarian and logistical assistance to the Haitian police and Coast Guard 2) create a safe environment for NGOs and other international organizations that were providing assistance to the Haitian people, and 3) work with other security agencies to stop the further deterioration of Haïti's precarious political state (Kirgis, 2004). Three months after the deployment of this MIF, acting on the recommendations of its Secretary-General (i.e., Kofi Annan), the UN sent its own peacekeeping corps to Haïti by launching a mission known as the United Nations Stabilization Mission in Haiti (Mission des Nations Unies pour la stabilisation en Haïti, or MINUSTAH).

On December 14, 2004, the leaders of MINUSTAH began their organization's peace- keeping mission by ordering hundreds of troops to move into a gang-controlled shantytown of Port-au-Prince named Cité Soleil (English: Sun City). With support from the Haïtian National Police (Police Nationale d'Haïti, or PNd'H), they succeeded in taking control of this slum area without encountering any serious resistance and having to kill any civilians or rebels (United Nations, 2005). By providing some security to Haïti's population, the soldiers of MINUSTAH allowed many Haïtians to resume their daily activities and made the provision of humanitarian assistance less life-threatening. Despite their early success, many Haïtians in Haïti and abroad criticized MINUSTAH for being largely ineffective. After they spread themselves around the country, insecurity continued to prevail as the rebels and other outlaws kidnapped and/or killed more civilians. In addition, MINUSTAH faced criticism for failing to investigate allegations of human rights abuses committed by members of the PNd'H. These violations consist of many gruesome acts. They span "from arbitrary arrest and detention, to disappearances and summary executions, to [the] killing of scores of hospitalized patients and the subsequent disposal of their bodies at mass graves" (Harvard Law Student Advocates for Human Rights and Centro de Justiça Global, 2005). Given MINUSTAH's failure to investigate and punish the perpetrators of these acts, some members of the interim government complained that its presence in Haïti was unwarranted.

Overall, in terms of corruption, the interim government fared relatively well. As aforementioned, not only did it put in place the ULCC —a major anti-corruption agency —it struggled with only a handful of small corruption scandals during its existence. In contrast to this claim, in January of 2005, a commission organized by the FL accused the Alexandre/Latortue government of being extremely corrupt. According to the members of this group, "In only 10 months, it broke all the records" of corruption in Haïti's history of more than 200 years (Freedom Archives, 2005) To support this outlandish claim, they cited, among other events, the following four scandals: 1) the fuel scandal at the National Palace, 2) the rice scandal at Latortue's Office,

3) the cases of corruption at several city halls and at the National office of Old Age Insurance, 3) embezzlement at the National Credit Bank of Cap-Haïtian, and 4) the diversion of humanitarian aid (Freedom Archives, 2005). Given this commission's unwavering loyalty to Aristide and its members' desire to see him return to power, some Haïtians questioned or dismissed these allegations.

In general, some Haïtians rejected the above accusations because they were largely placated by the fact that Latortue took steps to penalize all of the members of his office who Aristide loyalists claimed were culpable. For instance, some became somewhat appeased after learning that "The director of [his] cabinet, Raymond Lafontant, and his spokesperson, Michel Joseph, were suspended" (HaitiAction.net, 2005). Similarly, Amos Durosier —the leader of the ULCC —declared that "the Prime

Minister's collaboration in this matter has been exemplary" (HaitiAction.net, 2005). Given this sentiment of satisfaction in Haïti at the time, it is very likely that the claims of the FL commission were likely nothing more than inflammatory overstatements.

In the pages that follow, this work will not discuss the claims made the FL commission in greater depth for three important reasons. First, such an evaluation would cause the thesis to deviate from its aforementioned aim —which is to assess the ULCC's effectiveness by examining Haïti's level of corruption during the tenures of two presidents, one of Aristide's and the other of Préval's. Second, because the Alexandre/Latortue regime was a government that was impermanent and non-autonomous, it is likely that the ULCC's efforts during this period were excessively influenced by the international community. Third, it must be noted that there are only a handful of articles written on the aforesaid scandals. Because of this scarcity, any conclusions reached through an evaluation of the ULCC's activities would largely be based on speculations.

Préval's Second Tenure

During Préval's tenure in office, the GoH faced several serious cases of corruption. Months after assuming the presidency, Préval "identified [Haïti's] fight against corruption as a major priority, demanding full disclosure of financial records for top government officials" (Freedom House, 2011). In addition, he took immediate steps to ensure that corruption would become less rampant in Haïti. For instance, to bring down the level of corruption in the country's public and private sectors, his administration started an aggressive anti-fraud campaign in 2007. After Préval's regime launched this crusade, the GoH imprisoned several Customs employees who allegedly conspired to commit fraud (Global Security, n.d.). Similarly, on a more significant note, law enforcement officials imprisoned former board members of a bank named the Caribbean Banking Society (Société Caraïbéenne de Banque, or SOCABANK) for their involvement in the embezzlement of the bank's assets three years earlier. Known as the SOCABANK affair, this case quickly became a sensation in Haïti when its details became public.

Scandal 1

In order to determine if the ULCC and other governmental organizations played an effective role in combatting corruption during Préval's second term in office, this work aims to first examine a popular corruption allegation that troubled that the National Office of Pension Insurance (Office National d'Assurance Vieillesse, or ONA). In September of 2008, the ONA found itself in the middle of a money laundering and embezzlement scandal. During the course of that month and the next, public funds went towards buying luxurious gifts and providing big loans to the benefit of ONA officials (National Human Rights Defense Network, 2008a). For instance, an unidentified person purchased a USD 25,000 car in cash under the name of a woman who some people said had ties to Jacques Ketant —the aforementioned narcotrafficker who served as the godfather of one of Aristide's daughters before his imprisonment. Fundamentally, these acts of monetary misuse were illegal because they violated the anti-money laundering law adopted during Aristide's second term in office. The law in question forbids public officials from paying private enterprises cash amounts that exceed USD $5,000 without providing precise information on the origin of such large sums (Radio Kiskeya, 2008).

After investigating this scandal, the ULCC drafted and presented a report to the Prosecutor of the Port-au-Prince Court of First Instance. Although the Court agreed with the findings in the investigative report, it took no legal action against the perpetrator of the crimes. To explain the reason behind this judicial anomaly, an eminent Haïtian journalist named Nancy Roc claims that "According to trustworthy sources, President Préval interrupted the inquiry when he discovered that his sister had received a loan from ONA" (Roc, 2009). Whether this allegation is true or false, it shows that whereas the ULCC is willing to investigate some scandals, it refuses to enforce the consequences of its findings. Such a defect is systematically debilitating as it fails to deter money launderers and others who engage in other corrupt practices.

Scandal 2

During Préval's second tenure, "the Lavaud Scandal" was another major event that troubled the GoH. This affair began after Haïtian authorities arrested and extradited a notorious drug dealer named Alain Désir to the U.S. to face drug trafficking charges. On October 23, 2008, after searching the narcotrafficker's two homes, a group of law enforcement officers and magistrates seized some of Desir's possessions and sealed off his two properties. Shortly after this initial search, an unidentified person made authorities aware of the latter's possession of a large sum of money. With this new information in hand, authorities then searched the home of Marc Frederic —who not only was Alain Désir's uncle but also possessed a home in the same area. According to a report authored by Police Chaplains International, this second search became an operation of plunder. With the exception of the MINUSTAH official present at the time, Haïtian law enforcement officials stole several valuable items from Frederic's home and, most importantly, stole a sum of USD 10 to 32 million (Roc, 2009).

Upon learning about this incident, many Haïtians became outraged. To make matters worse, "Marc Frederic, was victim to an assassination attempt by four (4) armed individuals. After being shot in the stomach, he needed immediate surgical intervention. The attack confirmed that this dangerous case merit[ed] close attention from the Haitian authorities" (National Human Rights Defense Network, 2008b). Despite this fact, like it dealt with the ONA affair, Préval's administration was largely unresponsive. Although his regime removed several members of the Port-de-Paix justice system from their posts, it did not seek to deter future criminals by convicting any of the parties involved. As it did to the ULCC in the ONA affair, it devalued the efforts of the fact-finding organizations whose leaders took steps to determine if corrupt acts had taken place.

Chapter 6
Conclusion

Transparency International's Ranking of Haïti's Corruption Level

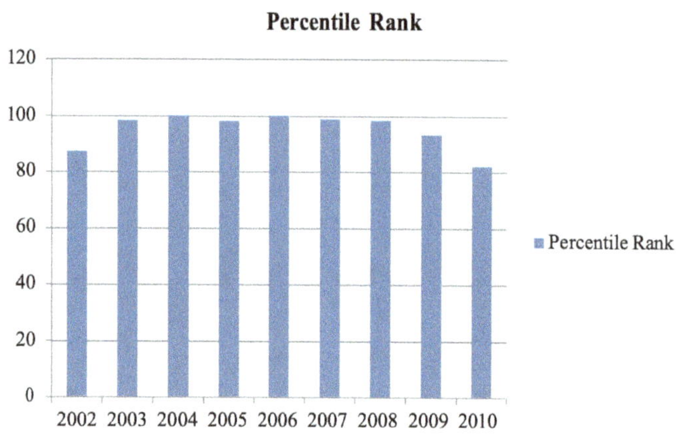

Source: I constructed this graph using data from TI's yearly Corruption Perceptions Index. According to TI, their Index "ranks countries/territo-

> ries based on how corrupt their public sector is perceived to be. A country/territory's score indicates the perceived level of public sector corruption on a scale of 0 - 10, where 0 means that a country is perceived as highly corrupt and 10 means that a country is perceived as very clean. A country's rank indicates its position relative to the other countries/territories included in the index."

Despite its examination of the actions of the ULCC in the preceding pages, this work has failed to discover if the organization's actions have succeeded in lowering Haïti's level of corruption. Although it shed some light on the activities of the institution, much remains to be learned about the effectiveness of the measures that it has adopted. Sadly, because the activities of organization are largely unreported in the literature and in Haïtian media, it is hard, if not impossible, to comprehensively assess how its actions have influenced Haïti's fight against corruption. In the chart above, because Haïti's ranks fluctuate, one therefore cannot rely on it to argue that the actions of the ULCC have had an effect on Haïti's level of corruption. Unsurprisingly, the chart below —which I constructed using data obtained from the World Bank's Worldwide Governance Indicators project —tells a somewhat similar story.

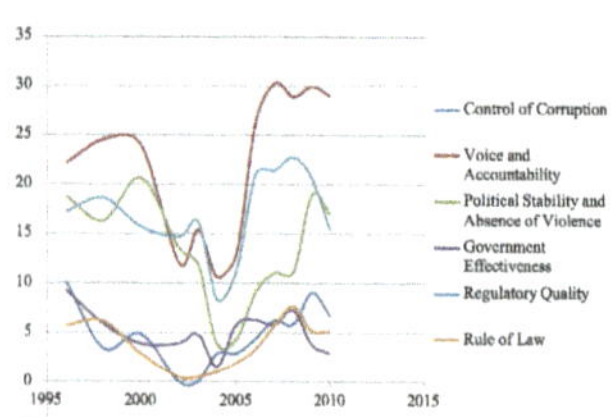

N.B.: In this graph, high x values correspond to superior levels of governance.

In this figure, most of the dimensions of governance not only increased after 2004 —the year during the founding of the ULCC —but also went beyond the previous peak levels that Haïti experienced during the late 1990s. In the face of this fact —owing to a lack of data —this work still cannot say for certain that the founding of the ULCC had a positive effect Haïti's level corruption. However, as mentioned above, because the leaders of the ULCC failed to persuade the GoH to prosecute several criminals when it had the chance to, one can vaguely conclude that its actions were ineffective.

In order to combat corruption, Haïti's leaders should draw on the works on many of the scholars mentioned above, in the literature review. For instance, they should draw on the works of Klitgaard and others to call for decentralization of the country's government and the establishment of strict monitoring systems and command structures that are more transparent and accountable. Similarly, others should borrow from the works of several rule of law advocates (e.g. Carothers) to urge their colleagues to improve their enforcement efforts and put in place different laws. Overall, any anti-corruption measure adopted by the GoH should be multi-dimensional. As aforementioned, corruption is so prevalent in Haïti that no one-dimensional solution will suffice to significantly lower the pervasiveness of the phenomenon within the country's government.

Chapter 7
References

Aidt, T. (2003). Economic Analysis of Corruption: A Survey. The Economic Journal, 113 (November), 632-652.

Anderson, C. (2012, February 21). Ex-Haitian Drug Lord Beaudoin 'Jacques' Ketant Could See Sentence Cut By Miami Judge. Huffpost Miami. Retrieved March 1, 2012, from http://www.huffingtonpost.com/2012/02/21/ex-haitian-drug-lord- beau_n_1290353.html

Arezki, R., & Brückner, M. (2009). Oil Rents, Corruption, and State Stability: Evidence From Panel Data Regressions (IMF Working Paper No. 09/267). Retrieved from International Monetary

Fund website: http://www.imf.org/external/pubs/ft/wp/2009/wp09267.pdf

Aristide Foundation for Democracy (n. d.). Learn More About AFD History. Retrieved March 9, 2012, from http://aristidefoundationfordemocracy.org/about/

Balot, R. (2001). Greed and injustice in classical Athens. Princeton: Princeton University Press.

Barclay, W. (1975). The daily study Bible series (Rev. ed.). Philadelphia: Westminster.

Barry-Shaw, N. (2007, June 26). Haiti: The Politics of Drugs. The Dominion. Retrieved March 1, 2012, from http://www.dominionpaper.ca/weblogs/nik_barry_shaw/1256 BBC News (2001, February 7). Aristide sworn in as Haiti's president.

BBC News. Retrieved February 10, 2012, from http://news.bbc.co.uk/2/hi/americas/1156540.stm

Beck, P., & Maher, M. (1986). A comparison of bribery and bidding in thin markets. Economic Letters, 20(1), 1-5.

Berryman, P. (1987). Liberation theology: essential facts about the revolutionary movement in Latin America--and beyond. New York: Pantheon Books.

Boycko, M., Shleifer, A., & Vishny, R. (1996). A theory of privatization. Economic Journal, 106(435), 309-19.

Brown, S. (2005, July 15). Aristide Foundation for Democracy's Questionable Business Transactions Revealed (fwd). {Web log post}. Retrieved February 8, 2012, from http://www.webster.edu/~corbette/haiti-archive-new/msg26032.html

Cable News Network (2004, February 24). Aristide warns more Haitians will become boat people.

Cable News Network. Retrieved March 1, 2012, from http://www.latinamericanstudies.org/haiti/warns.htm

Cameron, S. (2007). Caribbean Islands (17th ed.). Bath, England: Footprint.

Cédric, F. (2011, December 19). Facebook interview.

Charles, J., & Weaver, J. (2006, July 2). Drug Probe Targets Aristide. Le Nouvelliste. Retrieved March 1, 2012, from http://www.lenouvelliste.com/article.php?PubID=1&ArticleID=31386

Cupit, G. (2000). When Does Justice Require Impartiality? Paper for the Political Studies Association, UK 50th Annual Conference 10-13 April. Retrieved October 10, 2011, from http://www.psa.ac.uk/cps/2000/Cupit%20Geoffrey.ps.pdf

Deibert, M. (2005). Notes from the last testament: the struggle for Haiti (A Seven Stories Press 1st ed.). New York: Seven Stories Press.

Dodds, P. (2009, February 11). Haiti Swears In New Cabinet. CBS NEWS. Retrieved March 1, 2012, from http://www.cbsnews.com/2100-202_162-598583.html

Epatko, L. (2004, March 11). Rebuilding a Government. Public Broadcasting Service. Retrieved March 1, 2012, from http://www.pbs.org/newshour/bb/latin_america/haiti/rebuild.html

Farmer, P. (1994). The uses of Haiti. Monroe, ME: Common Courage Press.

Farmer, P., Fawzi, M., & Nevil, P. (2003). Unjust embargo of aid for Haiti. The Lancet, 361(9355), 420-423. Retrieved February 8, 2012, from http://www.thelancet.com/journals/lancet/article/PIIS0140-6736%2803%2912380- X/fulltext#article_upsell

Fatton, R. (2002). Haiti's predatory republic: the unending transition to democracy. Boulder, CO: Lynne Rienner

Publishers. Freedom House. (2011). Haiti | Freedom in the World 2011.

Freedom House. Retrieved March 5, 2012, from http://www.freedomhouse.org/report/freedom-world/2011/haiti

Freedom Archives (2005). {News} Chavez compares overthrow of Aristide to events in Venezuela {Web log post}. Retrieved March 3, 2012, from http://mail.freedomarchives.org/pipermail/news_freedomarchives.org/2005-February/000956.html

Gill, S. S. (1998). The pathology of corruption. New Delhi: Harpercollins Publishers India.

Global Security. (n.d.). Haiti – Corruption. GlobalSecurity.org – Reliable Security Information. Retrieved March 10, 2012, from http://www.globalsecurity.org/military/world/haiti/corruption.htm

Gonzalez, D. (2002, July 26). A Get-Rich Scheme Collapses, Leaving Haiti Even

Poorer. New York Times. Retrieved February 10, 2012, from http://www.nytimes.com/2002/07/26/world/a-get-rich-scheme-collapses-leaving-haiti-even-poorer.html?pagewanted=all&src=pm

HaitiAction.net (2005). HAITI: Corruption in the Coup Government and their own Rice Scandal. Retrieved March 3, 2012, from http://www.haitiaction.net/News/AHP/2005/01/26/02.html

Haïti Progrès (1996, February 21). Préval Taps Compromise Candidate for Prime Minister. Haïti Progrès. Retrieved February 8, 2012, from http://www.williambowles.info/haiti-news/archives/21270296.html

Haïti Progrès (2000, September 7). New Parliament faces mounting challenges.

Haïti Progrès. Retrieved February 8, 2012, from http://www.hartford- hwp.com/archives/43a/240.html

Hallward, P. (2004). Option Zero in Haiti. New Left Review, 27, 23-47. Retrieved February 10, 2012, from http://newleftreview.org/A2507

Hallward, P. (2007, February 22). An Interview with Jean-Bertrand Aristide. London Review of Books, 29, 9-13. Retrieved January 6, 2012, from http://www.lrb.co.uk/v29/n04/peter-hallward/an-interview-with-jean-bertrand-aristide

Hare, R. (2011). Moral Conflicts. The Tanner Lectures on Human Values (pp. 169-194). Cambridge, UK: Cambridge University Press. (Original work published 1980).

Harvard Law Student Advocates for Human Rights and Centro de Justiça Global (2005). Keeping the Peace in

Haiti? An Assessment of the United Nations Stabilization Mission in Haiti Using Compliance with its Prescribed Mandate as a Barometer for Success. Retrieved March 4, 2012, from http://www.law.harvard.edu/programs/hrp/documents/haitireport.pdf

Heidenheimer, A.J. (1970). Introduction. In A. J. Heidenheimer (Ed.), Political corruption: Readings in comparative analysis (pp. 2–28). New Brunswick NJ: Transaction Books.

Hopkin, J., & Rodriguez-Pose, A. (2007). "Grabbing hand" or "helping hand"? Corruption and the economic role of the state. Governance, 20(2), 187-208.

Huntington, S.P. (1968). "Modernization and Corruption." Political Order in Changing Societies, (New Haven: Yale University Press), 59-71.

Inter-Parliamentary Union (2000). HAITI: Parliamentary Elections Sénat, 2000.

Parliamentary Democracy - Inter-Parliamentary Union (IPU). Retrieved January 8, 2012, from http://www.ipu.org/parline-e/reports/arc/2138_00.htm

International Money Laundering Information Network (n.d.). Texte de la Loi du 21 février 2001 relative au blanchiment des avoirs provenant du trafic illicite de la drogue et d'autres infractions graves. Retrieved January 8, 2012, from https://www.imolin.org/amlid/showLaw.do?law=4639&language=FRE&country=HA I&print=yes

Isidor, Y. (2001, May). What's awaiting radical leftist Aristide ... the ultracautious man? Retrieved from http://www.wehaitians.com/what%27s.html

Karl, T. (2003). The Oil Trap. Transparency International Quarterly Newsletter, 9. Retrieved January 4, 2012, from http://www.transparency.org/publications/newsletter/editions

Kirgis, F. (2004). Security Council Resolution on Multinational Interim Force in Haiti. The American Society of International Law Home Page. Retrieved March 4, 2012, from http://www.asil.org/insigh128.cfm

Klitgaard, R. E. (1988). Controlling corruption. Berkeley: University of California Press.

Kurer, O. (2005). Corruption: An alternative approach to its definition and measurement. Political Studies, 53(1), 222-239.

Lebowitz, L. (2004, February 26). Drug dealer accuses Aristide. The Miami Herald. Retrieved March 1, 2012, from http://www.latinamericanstudies.org/haiti/ketant.htm

Leys, C. (1965). What is the Problem about Corruption? The Journal of Modern African Studies, 3(2), 215-230.

Lui, F. (1985). An Equilibrium Queuing Model of Bribery. Journal of Political Economy, 93(4), 760-781.

McGirr, S. (2011, February). Corruption, Anti-Corruption, and Political Competition. Prepared for University of Michigan Comparative Politics Workshop. Retrieved October 14, 2011, from http://sitemaker.umich.edu/comparative.speaker.series/files/cpw_w11_mcgirr.pdf

Morrell, J. R. (2000). Haiti Elections. Haiti Democracy Project. Retrieved March 8, 2012, from http://www.haitipolicy.org/archives/Publications&Commentary/snatch2.htm#N_1_

National Human Rights Defense Network. (2008a). Violation of the Right to Personal Liberty {Press Release}. Retrieved March 4, 2012, from http://www.rnddh.org/article.php3?id_article=400

National Human Rights Defense Network. (2008b). Scandal in the Justice System: A Call to Respect the Law and Raise the Moral Standards of Judicial and Police Practices. Retrieved March 4, 2012, from http://www.rnddh.org/IMG/pdf/Lavaud_Scandal.pdf

New York Times (1999, January 13). Haiti Leader to Rule by Decree; an Attack Follows. New York Times. Retrieved February 8, 2012, from http://www.nytimes.com/1999/01/13/world/haiti-leader-to-rule-by-decree-an-attack- follows.html

Nye, J. (1967). Corruption and Political Development: A Cost-Benefit Analysis. American Political Science Review, 61(2), 417-427.

Organization of American States. (2001, February 6). Third Report of the Mission of the Organization of American States to Haiti: Visit of the Assistant Secretary General to Haiti. Retrieved from http://www.oas.org/OASpage/Haiti_situation/02062001_eng.htm#II.%20THE%20 OAS%20AND%20HA%C3%8FTIS%20ELECTIONS%20IN%202000

Organization of American States. (2000, August 23). Report of the Mission of the OAS to Haiti. Retrieved from http://www.oas.org/xxxiiga/english/docs_en/report_Haiti.htm

Peters, J. G., & Welch, M. (2001). Gradients of Corruption in Perceptions of American Public Life. In A. J. Heidenheimer & M. Johnston (Eds.), Political corruption: Concepts and contexts (3rd ed.) (pp. 155-172). New Brunswick: Transaction Publishers.

Polgreen, L. (2004, March 10). A Premier Is Picked in Haiti; Marines to Disarm Militants. New York Times. Retrieved March 1, 2012, from http://www.nytimes.com/2004/03/10/world/a-premier-is-picked-in-haiti-marine

s - t o - disarm-militants.html?ref=gerardlatortue

Radio Kiskeya. (2008, September 29). Rebondissement dans l'Affaire Parquet de Port-au-Prince/ Judith Benoît: l'ULCC sollicite la mise en mouvement de l'action publique contre le directeur de l'ONA, Sandro Joseph. Retrieved March 4, 2012, from http://radiokiskeya.com/spip.php?article5295

Radio Métropole (2005, March 23). Installation du Bureau de réparation des sociétaires victimes . Radio Métropole. Retrieved February 14, 2012, from http://www.metropolehaiti.com/metropole/full_une_fr.php?id=9797

Rahman, A. (1986). Legal and administrative measures against bureaucratic corruption in Asia. Bureaucratic corruption in Asia--causes, consequences, and controls (pp. 147- 152). Quezon City: JMC Press.

Roc, N. (2009). Haïti: les raisins amers de la corruption. FRIDE. Retrieved March 4, 2012, from http://www.fride.org/download/COM_Haiti_Bitter_grapes_FRA_mar09.pdf

Rose-Ackerman, S. (2000). Is Leaner Government Necessarily Cleaner Government? In J. Tulchin and R. Espach (Eds.),Combating corruption in Latin America (pp. 87-106). Baltimore: Johns Hopkins Univ. Press.

Rose-Ackerman, S. (2008). Corruption. Readings in public choice and constitutional political economy (pp. 551-556). New York: Springer.

Rothstein, B. (2011). Anti-corruption: the indirect 'big bang' approach. Review of International Political Economy, 18(2), 228-250.

Shleifer, A., & Vishny, R. (1994). Politicians and firms. Journal of Economic Perspectives, 109(4), 995-1026.

Shleifer, A., & Vishny, R. (1998). The grabbing hand: government pathologies and their cures. Cambridge: Harvard University Press.

Teorell, J. (2007). Corruption as an Institution: Rethinking the Nature and Origins of the Grabbing Hand. The Quality of Government Institute, 5(November).

The 1987 Constitution of Haïti, art. 149. Retrieved March 1, 2012, from http://pdba.georgetown.edu/constitutions/haiti/haiti1987.html

The Republic of Haiti and Telecommunications D'Haiti, S.A.M. v. Jean-Bertrand Aristide, Faubert Gustave, Rodnee Deschineau, Lesly Lavelanet, Fred Beliard, Alphonse Inevil, Jean Rene Duperval, Adrian Corr, and Mont Salem Management, LTD. Retrieved February 2, 2012, from http://www.haitipolicy.org/Filed%20Complaint.pdf

The United States Department of Justice, Office of Public Affairs. (2011). Two Telecommunications Executives Convicted by Miami Jury on All Counts for Their Involvement in Scheme to Bribe Officials at State-Owned Telecommunications Company in Haiti {Press release}. Retrieved March 1, 2012, from http://www.justice.gov/opa/pr/2011/August/11-crm-1020.html

Thomas, M. A., and Patrick Meagher. 2004. A Corruption Primer: An Overview of Concepts in the Corruption Literature. Iris Discussion Papers on Institutions & Development no. 04/03. College Park, MD: Center for Institutional Reform and the Informal Sector, University of Maryland.

Transparency International. (2010). Frequently asked questions (GAQs). Transparency International. Retrieved February 8, 2012, from http://www.transparency.org/policy_research/surveys_indices/cpi/2010/faqs

Treisman, D. (2000). The causes of corruption: a cross-national study. Journal of Public Economics, 76(3), 399-457.

United Nations (2005). Report of the Secretary-General on the United Nations Stabilization Mission in Haiti. Retrieved March 4, 2012, from http://minustah.org/pdfs/rapportsSG/RSGFeb05.pdf Werner, S. (1983). New directions in the study of administrative corruption. Public Administration Review, 43(2), 146-154.

Chapter 8

First Peer Review Report

Peer-to-peer review about Law & Hoarders: Organized Crime and Corruption in Haiti

Introduction

First of all, I would like to introduce myself as an expert on the subject. My name is Mariane Trevisan, I am a Bachelor of Laws and a Lawyer, specialized in International Law by the Brazilian Law School (EBRADI), with professional experience and several articles published on Human Rights and International Law. During my undergraduate studies, I worked in several public agencies; the most relevant for this research were my internship at the Public Defender's Office of the State of São Paulo, where I worked as a trainee in Criminal Enforcement, and my internship at Public Prosecutor's Office of the State of São Paulo, where I worked as a trainee in Criminal Enforcement as well. Furthermore, in 2022 I had an article about Human Rights approved and presented at the Universidad Complutense in Madrid, in Spain. I am fluent in Portuguese and

English, and Spanish and French at advanced levels.

The present project demonstrates its pertinence already in the title, in which it provokes a curiosity in the reader by associating hoarder to organized crime and corruption in Haiti. However, after reading the whole book and returning to the title, I believe that it ended up being a little vague, despite arousing the reader's curiosity.

The peer-to-peer review that I am writing will be based on two main aspects: (1) the substance of the work, making some notes on possible improvements that would help give the project a greater scientific and legal basis and (2) the quality of its translation from English to French.

I - Introduction of the book

The author brings all the political background and cases that have led to cases of corruption over the years and governments in Haiti, which did not bear much relation to the title. I believe it would be more coherent to have a title that pointed, in some way, to the political scenario that will be addressed in the text.

In the introduction of the book, the author brings an important historical background, which I particularly like, because I believe it is important to situate and contextualize the reader in the time-space in which the reported facts occurred, which in this case are the acts of corruption, and situate him/her to the place of the facts, Haiti, and many times the reader will be in another country and may not have enough knowledge of the historical and political situation of the country.

Also in the introduction, the author states that he will discuss the measures adopted and their effectiveness in reducing corruption in Haiti. I see this as an important point because he shows the reader that he will not only explain the cases that occurred, but will have a critical view of what actually worked to eradicate the problem or not. In addition, the author brings that the study is unprecedented under the chosen viewpoint, which further evidences its pertinence within the academic diapason.

II - Development - Literature Review

At the beginning of the development of the book, the author brings interesting separation to analyze the literature that exists on the subject, but I believe it could have been placed with more topics, separating what each author says, and not just starting new paragraphs. This ensures that the text is easier to understand and does not become tiresome.

I believe it is also important to conceptualize and bring the problematic of the crimes of corruption relating them to White-Collar crimes, since, many times, the acts of corruption are committed by people who are in power, such as politicians, for example, and what will be demonstrated further on in the text.

I bring here a brief conceptualization of what would be the White-Collar crimes. According to the Corporate Finance Institute:

> "White-collar crime is a non-violent crime where the primary motive is typically financial in nature. White-collar criminals usually occupy a professional position of power and/or prestige, and one that commands well above average compensa tion.'' [1]

The term "white-collar" was coined by sociologist and criminologist Edwin Sutherland in the 1930s. This classification was a divider because people from high society were considered incapable of committing crimes, leaving these acts only to the marginalized population of a certain place.

This type of crime can be classified into individual crimes and crimes committed by criminal organizations.

It is related to the cases that will be discussed in the text for two reasons: (1) we will see cases committed by one person, but who hid and was part of a large criminal organization, which not only committed crimes of corruption, but was also involved in crimes of international drug trafficking; (2) it brings to the reader the demystification of the fallacy that only poor people are susceptible to commit crimes, but also and mainly people with great purchasing power, who hold the power of a country in their hands.

Such offenders who have greater financial conditions, when committing crimes, generate incredibly greater damage to the community than a poor person who commits such a crime, for example, as we will see in Case Study 2.

I would also like to bring, after bringing the White-collar conception, the other side of the coin: the corruption crimes committed by people who do not have so many financial conditions and what would lead to crime for these people.

An important issue that could be more addressed in the text concerns the sociological question. Mainly (but not only) in underdeveloped countries, as is the case of Haiti, the low remuneration of people, the lack of presence of the State in several places where they should be, providing services to the population, such as security, health, education, and are not present, make it easier for people to succumb to the decline of corruption. Just as the author brings the data that countries with great economic and political instability, as is the case of

Haiti, are more susceptible to the occurrence of numerous cases of corruption.

However, I emphasize that we should not blame them for a mistake of the State, which fails to guarantee the minimum to give people a dignified existence.

If people who already have a great financial condition and prestige in society succumb to corruption, why then shouldn't people who often don't have the minimum guaranteed for their existence also succumb?

I make it clear that I am not defending corruption, I just wanted to provoke, and I believe that it should be further explored by the author, a sociological reflection on the subject.

Once again, I mention that I missed a greater separation of the topics, where, for example, I would separate the given concepts according to the positions that were adopted by each author of the literature cited.

The author's statement about the philosopher Aristotle in the following quote is very pertinent:

> "Owing to the Aristotelian belief that human beings are by nature political creatures and the argument that impartial moral behavior requires "superhuman powers of thought, superhuman knowledge and no human weaknesses" (Hare, 2011, p. 182), impartiality within a political milieu is non-achievable."

Bringing philosophy as a point where one tries to conceptualize "corruption" and its nuances is important to escape the obvious, bringing a view from another area of human science. Sometimes, as in the case at hand and to conceptualize human behavior, for example, objective explanations are lacking. It is necessary to resort to other areas of human knowledge, as in this case, philosophy.

As placed above, after a conceptualization topic, and to guarantee, again, fluidity and not make the text tiresome for the reader, I would opt to open a new topic in which the writer would bring the focus that will be approached in the research, and the relation with the concepts of corruption already brought.

Brought in the same topic of "Literature Review", again, I would opt to separate with a new topic the explanations of the causes of corruption, according to the doctrine, and not just put it in another paragraph as was done. This makes it possible for the reader to get lost in the text.

Repeatedly, I point out as extremely pertinent the use of Aristotle's philosophy, and now also Plato's, to explain to the reader the causes of corruption. We can see this quote in the paragraph below:

> In terms of the specific causes of political corruption, the literature cites numerous factors as culprits. To begin with, ancient political philosophers such as Plato and Aristotle argue- -respectively in The Republic and Politics and Nicomachean Ethics--that societal inequality in its various forms along with human predisposition toward self-centeredness set forth the circumstances for corruption. According to these philosophers, as an aggressive type of materialistic acquisitiveness, greed (pleonexia in Greek) is a dangerous constituent of the human soul

(psuchê in Greek, or anima in Latin) (Balot, 2001).

Philosophy understands that corruption can be seen as something inherent in human nature, being the abuse of public or private power to obtain illicit advantages, contrary to the common good.

Facing the philosophical placement, I would like to add another suggestion to the author to make a paragraph, at least, citing the psychological perspective of corruption, such as, for example, what would lead people to delinquency, the questioning as to the existence of a character that would be evil and the exposure of the ego and to what extent this would influence the decision making of a person to commit something for his own benefit that would harm so many other people.

Another important point brought by the author is that democratic countries would be less susceptible to being harmed by corruption, because there is always alternation in power, with elections that take place after a certain period of time. Argument from the literature and that was well demonstrated by the author that it is not true, when presenting the cases brought, that elected presidents (and sometimes very popular in Haiti, like President Jean-Bertrand Aristide) were extremely corrupt too, as much as a dictator in another political regime.

Just to put the reader in context, President Aristide was not only accused of corruption, but also of facilitating drug trafficking, showing how big the problem can get.

In addition, I would like to point out the interesting problem of oil and the connection with corruption brought up at this point:

To make the point that certain economic milieus are more conducive to corruption than others, some development scholars contend that countries that obtain a large portion of their national income from oil-related commercial activities are frequently more corrupt than those without oil. For instance, Karl (2003) claims that oil-rich countries are often also governed more poorly, possess a culture of rent-seeking, and endure more incidences of civil conflict. In keeping with this assumption, once may surmise that the governments of such countries are more likely to be corrupt because they present their members with more opportunities for personal enrichment. Although Karl's conclu-

> sion seems logical, the empirical evidence on the correlation between the presence of economic rents, corruption, and political instability in oil-rich countries is remarkably scarce.

I emphasize this point because I believe that, like me, the reader has not paid attention or has not had this perspective. The author also points out the gaps in the study of oil-rich countries and that these have more cases of corruption, due to the economic importance of these countries and their political instability.

The author further brings that the literatures have cared little about the particular motives of individuals who commit corruption, because, according to them, it would be an individual behavior. Therefore, the author concludes that the literature has not yet exhausted all the biases necessary to understand the causes of corruption.

The author goes on to deal with anti-corruption measures, and which, I believe, should be in a separate topic, to allow more organization for the reader.

I point to a quote from the author:

> In addition, Ozfar (2007) urges systemically corrupt countries to change their laws so as to allow common citizens to file civil lawsuits against public officials whenever they neglect their duties or when they mismanage public funds (p. 264). Correspondingly, he also endorses a process called qui tam --a system through which private persons can file criminal charges against public servants for their role in corruption schemes (p. 264).

I would like to open a parenthesis to explain why, even in democratic societies, it would not be possible for civilians to denounce public officials in cases of non- compliance with their duties and corruption. First point: It would perhaps lead to accusations based on disaffection with the public official, with unfounded and revengeful accusations, aimed only at harming him. There would be too much discretion, in which it would not be known what the limit of this accusation would be, based only on real facts, avoiding any feeling of disagreement of the citizen with the public servant. It could also move the public machine for an investigation for a certain conduct and in the end be based on a dislike of the private individual, generating unnecessary costs to the public treasury, and could cause damages and greater expenses than the alleged corruption. The second point to be addressed would be who will judge the case. The judge could be conniving with the alleged corruption, because it is a co-worker who is being accused by a private individual, in an example of abuse of power of public corporativism.

The author brings a quote to counter the point of the suitability of the investigation that he brought above, which is:

> Ozfar thinks that the implementation of these two policies "could lead to a significant improvement in integrity in many systemically corrupt countries where the prosecutor's office has been compromised" (p. 261).

I refute this argument with the argument that many countries, especially the poorest ones, as mentioned above, have systems of prosecution that are as or more corrupt than the alleged accusation of corruption itself. For this reason, I believe that this argument is inefficient to remove the problem, being simplistic and disconnected with the factual reality of most countries.

After exposing the means to fight corruption, the author points out the failures of these means, especially in Haiti. Here, once again, I would make a separate topic, to improve the organization for the reader.

III - First Case Study

Excellent is the political historical contextualization of Haiti brought by the author. This contextualization allows the reader, who may often not know the history of the country. By showing that Jean- Bertrand Aristide, who was touted as the "messiah and savior of the homeland," declined his vast popularity in his second term as president of Haiti following accusations of corruption, collaboration for international drug trafficking, and facilitating the implementation of economic institutions in Haiti that were responsible for bankrupting much of the population.

By putting this into context and bringing it to the present day, it helps to better understand the roots of the problem. Here I would like to open another parenthesis for the phenomenon that has been observed in various parts of the world, but mainly in underdeveloped countries. The figure of a "savior", who would be above any mistakes and would be responsible for restoring the country and people's faith in an honest and transparent administration. Always populist speeches, which encompass themes such as the end of corruption and the repression of the corrupt, these figures aggravate the corruption situation, since they are always vectors of new corruptions, which will be discovered after their mandate in some cases, and further worsen the population's disbelief in a repair of the country. People find themselves deceived once again, but with the addition of having vehemently believed in that politician, which ends up pushing the population further and further away from an effective participation in the political life of the country.

By delving into the basis of this blind belief, we can point out that the lack of education is one of the primary causes for this phenomenon to occur. Providing quality education in Haiti, as in many underdeveloped countries, is not a priority for the government. Providing a quality education allows the population to acquire knowledge and develop critical thinking, enabling them to question governmental acts and increase vigilance over the political administration of elected officials.

The above is demonstrated in the topic "Scandal 2", for example, in which the government created financial institutions, the so-called CEC's, sponsored by the USA, with the consent of the then Haitian president, Aristide. The CEC's (Coopératives d'épargne et de credit, in French), the text itself says, would be an important instrument to guarantee a huge economic advance for the country. Investors were promised high and rapid returns, which caused thousands of Haitians to sell everything and spend their savings to invest in these institutions.

As the CECs collapsed, people revolted at the loss of so much money, and this was responsible for creating even more political instability in Haiti. After the

proper investigation, it was discovered the participation and profits obtained by the public agents of the country.

I also point out the great graphics placed by the author in the text. It allows a better visualization and understanding of the facts for the readers, especially for those who do not have specific knowledge about the subject.

Finally, in this case, the author brings an excellent analysis of the anti-corruption measures adopted and if they were effective in ending the problem. Concluding that they were not sufficient, the author gives the reader the full dimension of the problem and shed light on how systemic the corruption problem is.

IV - Second Case Study

This case is about the politics of reconstruction in Haiti and the possibility of an honest and transparent government led by Aristide's successor, Boniface Alexandre. Together with his prime minister, the renowned lawyer Gérard Latortue.

However, according to the ULCC, a major anti-corruption agency, the government was found to be extremely corrupt.

I found it extremely interesting that some Haitians did not believe the accusation that Alexandre's government was corrupt, because it was responsible for applying some punishment to the crimes of the former president, Aristide. This points out, once again, how a country that has not invested in education has its population easily manipulated. The feeling of satisfaction of the population for having punished someone, cancels out any other need to punish new corruptions.

V – Conclusion

Despite Haiti being the first nation to become independent in Latin America, being the oldest majority black republic, and being the second republic to be formed, behind only the United States, Haiti is the poorest country in Latin America, and one of the poorest in the world. Here I want to highlight, and I think it is important that it is also highlighted in the conclusion by the author, the harmful effect that corruption committed by politicians can have on its population.

Finally, in the conclusion, I believe the reader would expect a positive conclusion, that the anti-corruption measures adopted were efficient. It is very genuine that the author recognizes that it is difficult to reach a positive conclusion, mainly due to the lack of data and reported complaints and adequate investigations of the cases.

About the notes concerning the translation from English to French, it brought a cultured and objective language, which allows the reader to absorb the essence of what was studied by the author.

ENDNOTES:

[1] Available in https://corporatefinanceinstitute.com/resources/esg/white-collar-crime/

Chapter 9

Second Peer Review Report

PEER REVIEW: LAW & HOARDERS: ORGANIZED CRIME & CORRUPTION IN HAITI

I, Liisa Helmi Paultre, am a French lawyer and translator with a master's degree from the Sorbonne University in Paris with a double major in Law and Political

Science. I have worked as a legal advisor and translator for 10 years, mainly in the media and entertainment industry, and have a long history of volunteering for several non-governmental organizations. I was born and raised in France and Sweden, and I am trilingual in French, Swedish, and English.
I have written this review without knowledge of the author's identity. As the pronouns of the author are unknown to me, the pronouns "they" and "their" will be used in this review to refer to the author.

The work examines organized crime and corruption in Haiti during the presidency of Aristide and Préval by looking at the anti-corruption measures taken by the ULCC anti-corruption agency.

The Introduction gives a historical background to the political instability of Haiti since its birth as an independent nation. The indemnity Haiti must pay to France is cited as one of the reasons why Haiti is underdeveloped, although the details of such debt are not explained any further. The author goes into more detail regarding the ULCC agency's creation and its effects on corruption in Haiti. The issues raised by the author and the questions they will answer are cleverly laid out in this Introduction, although maybe the author should have asked a broader question considering the structure and content of the manuscript. It is interesting to read that the actions of the ULCC have never been analyzed by researchers before, which attracts the reader's curiosity. However, the author should maybe have brought up the difficulties of evaluating the effectiveness of the ULCC, e.g. the lack of reliable data, in the Introduction.

The author starts by exposing his methodology for the Literature Review, which consists of laying out the existing knowledge regarding the subject matter before assessing its accuracy. The lack of definition of the term "corruption" and its types of action is important here. The author manages to point out the flaws of the different proposed definitions, before explaining why the PAC model of Rothstein is the definition the author will use in their manuscript.

The author goes on to list the scholars who have worked on the reasons why corruption "arises and persists", going back as far as Socratic philosophers. The philosophical ground of modern governmental institutions is very interesting and beautifully laid out. The author goes on to criticize the fact that the particular factors of corruption, such as moral values and interpersonal dynamics, have been neglected by scholars. It is surprising to read that the author considers the scholars' approach to the issue too systemic. Such criticism is very unusual nowadays, as the academic world tends to lean towards a systemic approach for most subjects.

The author continues to explain the two opposing approaches among scholars: the systemic approach to corruption and the Rule of Law approach. Finally, the different solutions proposed to prevent corruption are laid out, such as legal reforms and NGOs. The efficacity of each such anti-corruption measure is carefully questioned by the author, and the literature's many flaws are laid out. The obstacles faced by anti-corruption agencies are laid out, together with an example of one of the few agencies that was successful: the ICAC. A comparison of the ICAC and the ULCC would have maybe been helpful in this section.

The author emphasizes their personal experience with the literature and Haitian culture to further make their hypothesis known. The author seems confident when laying out their hypothesis, and the author expects the author to have clear answers by the end of the manuscript.

Even if the author has chosen not to make a separate section to lay out their methodology, their approach and problematization are intelligible and coherent. The historical, philosophical, and economic background of the corruption problem in Haiti is crystal clear to the reader after reading the Introduction and Literature Review. The author will then further develop the political background of corruption, starting off with a First Case Study.

The reader is then presented with the First Case Study, introduced by a Political Background. The author's approach seems to be to evaluate the effectiveness of the ULCC by analyzing corruption before the creation of the ULCC in the First Case Study and after the creation of the ULCC in the Second Case Study.

The rise of Aristide, and his exile, as well as his return, is sometimes hard to follow. For example, it is first unclear what the author means when they write "Aristide once again took control of Haiti's presidency" (p.22): did he win the election or was it a military coup? Luckily, the author goes into more detail about the 2000's elections later in the First Case Study. Ultimately, the author manages to summarize a lot of Haiti's political history in this Political Background.

The first scandal is about the elections of May and July 2000, which has already been previously mentioned in the Political Background. The author summarizes all the events and manages to expose both sides' claims.

The second scandal is the pyramid scheme created by the cooperative banking institutions created by President Aristide. The horrible consequences this pyramid scheme had on Haitians are well presented by the author. The author gives personal insight into how it was to live in Haiti at the time of this scandal, creating a strong sense that the author has, from personal experience, a strong knowledge of the subject and an emotional attachment to the issue of corruption in Haiti.

The author goes on to list the Anti-Corruption Efforts taken by the UCREF and all the evidence of corruption they found when investigating the Aristide presidency. The difficulties and obstacles faced by Haiti to convict lawbreakers, and, therefore, the ineffectiveness of the anti-corruption agencies is made obvious here. The author explains that they want to determine if the anti-corruption measures taken before the creation of the ULCC were effective. The author could have made a more impactful point if the author had compared the UCREF and ULCC, and the way they operate, in a more straightforward way.

The First Case Study sometimes feels like a multitude of case studies: the first presidency of René Préval, two political scandals, anti-corruption efforts, etc. However, each political event is well-explained, with the author going into extensive details about the Haitian political system and its scandals.

The author uses maps and charts as a visual aid, making complex political scandals more intelligible to the reader. The First Case Study is dense, nonetheless, the author finds a way to captivate the reader's attention by telling the fascinating story of the many scandals in Haiti at the beginning of the 2000s.

The author manages to fully explain a very complex political situation and the many ways in which corruption has plagued Haiti. The inability to bring to justice politicians involved in corruption scandals is evident – only some drug dealers and narcotraffickers are convicted. Although the author needs to analyze the situation before the creation of the ULCC, it would have maybe been more balanced if the First Case Study was a bit shorter. Indeed, the

hypothesis of the author is barely touched on in the First Case Study. The lengthy details sometimes make it slightly difficult to follow the thread of the manuscript.

The Second Case Study is somewhat more concise and straightforward. The First Case Study gives a solid background to the Second Case Study, even if the division between the two case studies is a bit less coherent. The Second Case Study focuses on Préval's administration and the corruption scandals that shook Haiti in the late 2000s.

First, the author gives an overview of the interim government of Boniface Alexandre. The author describes the accusations of corruption this interim government faces as "outlandish" (p.47). The author chooses not to discuss such claims and the four alleged scandals supporting them and chooses to rather focus on the anti-corruption measures taken by the interim government.

The first scandal occurred during Préval's second term of office and involved money laundering. Once again, the government and the narcotraffickers were caught in embezzlement. The author stresses the failure of the ULCC to take legal action against the perpetrators of the crimes they discovered.

The second scandal, the "Lavaud Scandal", is also a scandal involving drug traffickers, and, once again, the parties involved were not convicted, leaving the reader flabbergasted by the ineffectiveness of the Haitian system. The author would have maybe benefitted from giving the reader more insight into the Haitian legal system to better understand this injustice.

The Second Case Study is brief but impactful. The readers are left with a bitter feeling of injustice by the end of this section. However, the author could have gone into more detail about the creation of the ULCC, its structure, and its course of action.

The conclusion starts off with an uncommon statement: "this work has failed to discover if the organization's actions have succeeded in lowering Haiti's level of corruption" (p.52). The failure of the author to determine through his work whether the ULCC has succeeded in lowering Haiti's corruption or not comes slightly as a shock to the reader, given the confidence of the author when laying out his hypothesis in the Introduction and Literature Review. Citing the lack of available sources, the author claims it is almost impossible to analyze the evolution of corruption in Haiti. The author even advises Haitian leaders to consult other scholars' work instead of their own. Still, the author "vaguely" (p.53) concludes that the ULCC's actions were ineffective. The term "vaguely" seems like an understatement, as the author has through his study very clearly broken down how the perpetrators of corruption crimes were never punished. Sadly, this conclusion minimizes the impact of the author's own work. Unfortunately, there is a clear contrast between the ambitions of the author in the Introduction and the pessimism of the Conclusion.

In general, the language of the author is very fluid and easy to follow. The vocabulary is rich, and the manuscript is overall very well written in both English and French. The author's tone is neutral throughout the work, although it is a difficult subject involving violence, corruption, and injustice. The author's personal experience living in Haiti never seems to cloud the author's judgment. The author uses "s/he" when speaking about a universal person, which creates a sense of inclusivity in the manuscript.

The translation is well-executed, if not flawless. It is difficult to identify the original language of the work, as both language versions are very eloquent. The charts are translated as well, as they were designed by the author, making them easier to read. However, some of the references in the French version were in both French and English, making it confusing to the reader (e.g. Hare, R. (2011) « Moral Conflicts. », p.123). Furthermore, the page numbers on the top right corner of the pages are incorrect in the French version of the references (p.120 to 128). Otherwise, the French translation is impeccable.

The Literature Review is well-referenced, but the manuscript could have cited more sources in the two case studies - even if the author emphasizes the lack of data and articles in the Conclusion. For example, there are very few articles and documents from French sources in the references, although Haiti is a French-speaking country.

The reader navigates through the history of corruption in Haiti in the late 1990s and 2000s and gets a very clear view of the political situation in Haiti during this period.
However, the author may have benefitted from making the two case studies more chronological and clearly divided – for example by adding a title to each case study - into two distinct periods: before the creation of the ULCC and after the creation of the ULCC. This would have also made reading the charts showing the evolution of corruption in Haiti easier.

The manuscript is sometimes a bit unbalanced. The author's work focuses on the work of the ULCC and its effect on corruption in Haiti. However, the First Case Study– which is also the lengthiest – retraces in detail events taking place before the creation of the ULCC in 2004. Although it is smart for the author to analyze the situation before the creation of the ULCC, this First Case Study feels slightly too long and sometimes too far from the point the author is trying to make.

To conclude, the manuscript lacks problematization in some parts of the manuscript, and the author fails to answer the questions the manuscript aspired to answer. This is regrettable, as the author put a lot of effort into giving the reader a rich historical and political background to corruption in Haiti. Indeed, the work sometimes feels more like a history of corruption in Haiti than a hypothesis. Maybe the author should have reshaped his work when faced with the lack of sources and statistics available to them - or used this obstacle to denounce the lack of transparency and effectiveness of anti-corruption agencies.

It is my opinion that the author would benefit from changing the angle and structure of his manuscript to be able to conclude it in a more impactful way.

Chapter 10

Third Peer Review Report

Peer Review Report of Attorney Camille Molina-Brusley

I am a practicing attorney. I was admitted to the Paris Bar in May of 2016 (nearly 7 years ago), have practiced law in Paris, and worked as a paralegal in New York. Educationally, I graduated from the Paris Bar School in 2015, after completing the School's professional training program. In addition, I graduated from the Sorbonne Law School, where I completed a master's degree in international criminal law (with honors) in 2011. Before Sorbonne, I was at the University of Kent, whence I obtained an English Law Diploma (with merit) in 2010, and attended Sorbonne Law School, whence I graduated with a bachelor's degree in law (with honors) in 2009. As a native French speaker who is also fluent in English and Spanish, I performed a double-blind review of this manuscript, *Law & Hoarders*.

The manuscript entitled "Law & Hoarders: Organized Crime & Corruption in Haiti" examines the particularly high level of corruption in Haiti. In order to do so, the author examines among other things the impact that may have had the *Unité de Lutte Contre la Corruption* (ULCC), a semi-autonomous Combat Unit against Corruption created in September of 2004 by the interim government of President Boniface Alexandre.

In order to study the impact of this institution on the level of corruption in the country, the manuscript focuses on several case studies, precisely on scandals that occurred during the second presidency of Jean-Bertrand Aristide on the one hand, and during the second presidency of René Préval on the other hand, these two governments being respectively the ones in power before and after the implementation of the ULCC. In particular, the manuscript examines two corruption scandals that occurred within each of these governments. At the end of this study, the author concludes that the level of corruption unfortunately does not seem to have decreased in Haiti following the creation of this anti-corruption institution.

This study was conducted in English and French, using sources in both languages, which will allow us to evaluate not only its content in the first instance, but also the quality of its translation in the second instance.

Before examining more specifically the different sections of the manuscript, it is possible to assert, from a general point of view, that this study should be praised in various aspects: the choice and the approach of the subject, the explanations given, which are clear and synthetic, and finally the thorough presentation of the cases. The elements of context and the specificities of the History of

Haiti necessary to the clarity of the study are perfectly explained, which allow the reader to take interest in the topic and to understand this otherwise difficult subject.

The introduction of the paper allows to identify very precisely the limits of the subject and the stake of the study. It also presents the institution of the ULCC and addresses some of the measures it has put in place in the fight against corruption.

The next section of the paper, entitled "literature review", examines the abundant doctrine surrounding the subject of corruption.

First, the manuscript rightly focuses on finding the suitable definition of “corruption”, which, as the author explains, is a difficult task to achieve, as corruption is a particularly equivocal notion. The paper goes through, in a very interesting and complete way, many suggestions for a fitting definition and an explanation of the most commonly used model, namely the "Principal-Agent-Client" (PAC) model.

Ideally, a good definition of corruption would allow to cover all the different forms of corruption: bribery, nepotism, embezzlement, influence peddling, and so on.

For the purpose of completing the information provided in the paper, it could be interesting to carry out a brief study of the laws incriminating corruption in the Haitian legislation, in order to know which corruption practices are authorized or, on the contrary, incriminated within the country's legislation. As well, it would be beneficial to go through the changes and

evolutions of these laws, such as the law of March 12, 2014 on the prevention and repression of corruption.

Similarly, it might also be interesting to look at the difference between active and passive corruption, and the importance of studying this behavior from two different angles: from the perspective of the corrupter and the one of the corrupted.

This same section then takes a very interesting look at the potential causes of corruption, and more specifically in the case of Haiti, identifying three main reasons: the high level of poverty, the existence of a dysfunctional national judicial system, and the lack of transparency in the various branches of the Haitian government.

Finally, this section is devoted to a brief review of anti-corruption measures, and tries to figure out whether these measures could be universal or need to be adapted more specifically to each place, due to differences of culture or to the specificities of each country.

The paper then addresses the first case study, which is the level of corruption during the presidency of Jean-Bertrand Aristide from 2000 to 2004, prior to the creation of the ULCC by the interim government of Boniface Alexandre and Gérard Latortue. To this end, the author clearly sets out the political and historical context of Haiti before presenting the first scandal that shook this government: the tax fraud scandal of 2000, in which President Aristide and members of his party obtained up to 92% of the votes.

The second scandal that hit the government of Jean-Bertrand Aristide was the so-called "pyramid scheme" in which large numbers of Haitians invested in *Coopératives d'Epargne et de Crédit* (CEC), which were supported and advertised by President Aristide, although they subsequently went bankrupt, resulting in losses estimated at over $200 million for the Haitian families that had invested in those companies.

The manuscript then examines the anti-corruption efforts made in the aftermath of these two scandals, prior to the creation of the ULCC. Despite the investigations conducted, notably by the *Unité Centrale de Renseignements Financiers* (UCREF) created by Aristide, none of the people involved in either of the two scandals were prosecuted or found liable, and it seems that the anti-corruption efforts have been more efficient in the United States than in Haiti.

Following the same pattern as the first case study, the manuscript focuses on the second study and looks at the level of corruption in the country following the establishment of the ULCC. After explaining the context of Alexandre's interim government and the presidency of René Préval, who made the fight against corruption a priority, the author highlights two major scandals that occurred during Préval's presidency from 2006 to 2011:

- The money laundering and embezzlement scandal that affected the *Office Nationale d'Assurance Vieillesse* (ONA), which did not lead to any legal proceedings despite the investigation report presented by the ULCC to the Prosecutor of the Port-au-Prince Court of First Instance,

- The "Lavaud scandal" involving the theft of more than $10 million by public officials during a police search.

Following the presentation of these two case studies, and more specifically of these four scandals, the manuscript concludes on the impact that the ULCC may have had on the level of corruption in Haiti. The author rightly appears to be very pessimistic about the effects of the ULCC on corruption, particularly because of the great impunity that remains regarding acts of corruption and organized crime.

In this aspect, and regarding the extent of corruption in Haiti, it might also be instructive to research whether the ULCC has received the means necessary to accomplish the task it has been assigned. For example, since the ULCC has no enforcement powers of its own, it is bound to hand in reports and make suggestions to the courts as to who should be prosecuted, but cannot itself prosecute the individuals identified as responsible.

Indeed, the study simply states that, as the level of corruption in Haiti appears to be unchanged, it is likely that the *Unité de Lutte Contre la Corruption* has had no significant impact since its creation in 2004. It might be interesting to supplement this work with some additional data on the institution of the ULCC. These could include but are not limited to:

- a description of its organization and functioning, which might explain why this institution has not reached the hoped-for results,
- the numbers and statistics relating to its activity,
- the reports that the ULCC could have issued, and so on...

In conclusion, this manuscript deals with a very interesting subject from a practical perspective, which deserves to be completed and updated, especially to examine the longer- term effects of anti-corruption efforts.

- The English expression "plea bargain" has been translated literally as "accord de plaidoyer", which does not really fit any process in French law; it would have been clearer to speak of "négociation de la peine" or "plaider-coupable" (see page 39).

- The expression "partners in crime" has been literally translated into French as "les partenaires d'Aristide dans le crime", whereas this expression has no equivalent in French; it might have been better to use the term "complice" or "acolyte" if one wanted to keep the colloquial connotation (see page 39).

There are also small inaccuracies in the translation which, unlike the examples given above, do not hinder the understanding of the text, but that could be improved. As an example, we can cite:

- The term "copinage", which is familiar in French, could be replaced by "favoritisme", the preferred expression to describe this criminal behavior (see page 1).

- The term "multi-country" is an anglicism that could be replaced by the word "multinational" (see page 2).

- In the translation of the sentence "as an aggressive type of materialistic acquisitiveness, greed (. ..) is a dangerous constituent of the human soul", the terms "acquisitiveness" and "greed" were replaced with the same word "avidité", instead of finding a synonym and thus avoiding an incorrect repetition (see page 9).

- The expression "shed some light" has been translated as "jeté une certaine lumière", while the idioms "mettre en lumière" or "faire la lumière sur" should have been preferred (see page 52).

These comments can be applied to the title of the manuscript. Indeed, while it is quite understandable that the title represents a pun in the English language, its translation does not work very well in French, and could render perplex a reader who does not understand the pun in English. Moreover, the expression "organized crime" normally corresponds to an expression that is enshrined in French law, namely "criminalité organisée", which should therefore have been preferred.

- Finally, it seems important to note a few minor translation errors:

- "Depuis sa défaite contre les Français" is a misunderstanding as the original text spoke of victory and not defeat (see page 1).

- The phrase "21 mai dernier" does not convey the same idea, meaning last 21st of May, whereas a date appears in the English text (see page 30).

- The translation "soit quatre fois plus que pendant son règne" is incorrect and means the opposite of the English sentence "a fourfold increase during {his} rule" (see page 40).´
  - The translation of the sentence "Compte tenu de la loyauté indéfectible de cette commission envers Aristide et du désir de ses membres de le voir revenir au pouvoir, certains Haïtiens se sont interrogés ou ont rejeté l'idée d'un retour au pouvoir." is not correct compared to the original version and, therefore, the part of the sentence underlined should be replaced by "ces allégations" (cf. page 47).

Apart from these few comments, the translation from English to French is quite satisfactory.